Master Ma's
Ordinary Mind

Master Ma's Ordinary Mind

The

Sayings

—— *of* ——

ZEN MASTER
MAZU DAOYI

by Fumio Yamada

Translated from Japanese by Nick Bellando

With an Appendix by Andy Ferguson

Wisdom Publications
199 Elm Street
Somerville, MA 02144 USA
wisdompubs.org

Library of Congress Cataloging-in-Publication Data
Names: Yamada, Fumio, 1959– author. | Bellando, Nick, translator.
Title: Master Ma's ordinary mind: the sayings of Zen Master Mazu Daoyi /
    by Fumio Yamada; translated from Japanese by Nick Bellando.
Other titles: Hajimete no zen mondō. English
Description: Somerville, MA: Wisdom Publications, 2017. | Includes index.
Identifiers: LCCN 2016030099 (print) | LCCN 2016049084 (ebook) |
    ISBN 9781614292814 (pbk.: alk. paper) | ISBN 1614292817 (pbk.: alk.
    paper) | ISBN 9781614293057 () | ISBN 1614293058 ()
Subjects: LCSH: Mazu, 709–788. | Zen Buddhism—Quotations, maxims,
    etc. | Zen Buddhism—China.
Classification: LCC BQ9550.H6592 M397913 2016 (print) | LCC
    BQ9550.H6592 (ebook) | DDC 294.3/927—dc23
LC record available at https://lccn.loc.gov/2016030099

ISBN 978-1-61429-281-4   ebook ISBN 978-1-61429-305-7

21 20 19 18 17
5 4 3 2 1

Cover design by Phil Pascuzzo. Interior design by
Kristin Goble. Set in Berling LT Std 10.5/14.5.

Wisdom Publications' books are printed on acid-free paper and meet
the guidelines for permanence and durability of the Production
Guidelines for Book Longevity of the Council on Library Resources.

❀ This book was produced with environmental mindfulness. For more
information, please visit wisdompubs.org/wisdom-environment.

Printed in the United States of America.

Please visit fscus.org.

Contents

Part III: Always Be Your True Self, Independent and Free

Part IV: *Your* Mind Is Buddha

Contents

Translator's Preface

Fumio Yamada's personality comes out in his writing. He's the sort of person who gives you room to explore, room to fail, room to succeed—room to be yourself. Whether or not you agree with his interpretations or ideas is beside the point; his aim is to learn with you, not to teach you.

Fumio and I have spent many hours discussing Zen and related topics together, exploring old things and letting them become new. The conversation always takes on a life of its own, wandering off the path, and sometimes ending up somewhere altogether different. As you walk through this text, you'll enjoy a similar dialogue. His own natural insight and sense of curiosity, coupled with his nearly forty years of working with Zen and classical Chinese, will bring out the human side of the sayings of Master Mazu—which is often lacking in English-language literature on the subject.

It is precisely this human side that makes Mazu such an attractive figure. While mulling over his dialogues with Fumio, I discovered a side of Zen that hadn't been so explicit in collections I'd read of other masters. Mazu isn't just about smacking people into reality and confounding them with riddles; instead, he speaks like someone who truly cares about the people who have been entrusted to him. He wants them to know that they are valuable just as they are—and once they understand that, he wants them to go even further, breaking down every obstacle and hindrance so that their personality flourishes fully, so that they can be truly alive.

That "life" that Mazu wants to nurture is still present in the text—which only really comes alive when you find yourself in it. Only then can the "past" contained in the text truly become "present." In reading this book, you will come into conversation with both Mazu Daoyi and Dr. Yamada—and hopefully with yourself as well.

Overall, this translation was made with the attempt to preserve the vibrancy of the original Zen dialogues as well as the dynamic between them and Dr. Yamada. Zen history is one of endless and layered encounter, from the one between Bodhidharma and the first Chinese Zen disciples to the ones you will have with this very text. These are your encounters. Whether they bring laughter, joy, warmth, or bewilderment, above all, may they inspire and draw out the wondrously valuable life that's in you.

Nick Bellando

Author's Preface

I wanted to make a map that would serve to guide people through the world of Master Mazu.

Whether a map is actually useable or not depends on the scale you use. If you try to draw it in perfect detail, it ends up growing to a scale of 1:1. Such a life-size map can hardly be said to be useable; on the other hand, if you make it as general and undetailed as a standard desktop globe, it doesn't prove to be of much practical use either.

If you walk along through the world of Master Mazu, using my map as a guide, you'll see all of the important sights without missing a thing. However, mine is not a conventional tourist map. When the popular sights don't seem very interesting, we simply pass them by. On the other hand, when we come to a place that I like, we take our sweet time, regardless of whether it's actually deemed a "sight" or not.

While walking along with Mazu, for instance, I'll lead you on several detours to visit people like Nanquan and Zhaozhou. We take a little breather with these gentlemen, and before we know it Mazu will already be walking way up ahead of us, so we must scramble and stumble along to catch up.

Make no mistake: This is not meant to be an analytical, academic work. If you are looking for source criticism and historical analysis, there are plenty of other texts that address these issues very skillfully. This book contains the personal reflections of an ordinary person—written for ordinary (and extraordinary) people.

My prayer is that, like a butterfly crossing the Sakhalin Strait, the words in this book will somehow reach the heart of the reader.

Fumio Yamada

Part I

Ordinary Life Is the Way

1

The Salt and Miso Are Not Lacking

Huairang, hearing that Mazu had begun teaching in the Jiangxi region, asked his disciples about it.

"Is Daoyi really expounding the Dharma for the masses?"

"Indeed he is."

"And no one came to tell me about it!"

Huairang sent one of the monks to see Mazu, telling him to wait until Mazu entered the Dharma hall to deliver his Dharma talk and then to ask him simply, "How's it going?" The monk was to remember whatever Mazu said in reply and then report back.

The monk went to see Mazu and did as he had been instructed. Mazu replied, "It's been thirty years since my dubious start; at present, salt and miso are not lacking."

The monk returned to Huairang and reported what he had heard.

Huairang approved.

讓和尚、聞師闡化江西、問衆曰、道一為衆説法否。衆曰、已為衆説法。讓曰、総未見　人持箇消息来。遂遣一僧往彼、俟伊上堂時、但問作麼生、待渠有語記取来。僧依教往問　之。師曰、自従胡乱後三十年、不少塩醬。僧回挙似讓。讓然之。

Mazu's response that "at present, salt and miso are not lacking" is quite interesting; it's perhaps as if he's saying, "I started out without any idea of what I was getting into, but thanks to your training, I'm not going hungry."

A rich lifestyle doesn't guarantee that you'll have peace of mind; too many possessions tend to invite suffering. But salt and miso are basic staples, so it would be acceptable to read this as the common sentiment that the happiest life is that of honest poverty. However, considering Huairang's interest in his former student, there may be something a bit deeper going on in the details.

In his response, perhaps Mazu is simply revealing his mind: "I'm just living everyday life. To live without artificial problems is Zen itself. No need to say anything more."

I suppose a Zen priest would be expected to have such an attitude, but those in the secular world might not find it so easy. A teacher in the midst of the bustle of worldly life, concerned with helping a hard-working student to find a job, might be tempted to say something to the tune of this: "'Just live naturally' is a nice ideal, but it won't put food on the table. You need to be practical. Settle for a desk job." But remembering

Mazu's words, he restrains himself, instead giving the following advice: "Go for it! Set your sights high, follow your dreams. It may be tough at first, but go ahead and live out the life that's in you." Perhaps Mazu's road to becoming a Zen master with his own temple wasn't easy, and that's what he calls his "dubious start." Thirty years later, he's made it—he's living his life to the fullest and hasn't failed to put food on the table.

A realized being seeks nothing, not even enlightenment. He or she can be completely satisfied with a simple diet of brown rice, miso soup, and vegetables. In Japan, this natural, no-problem way of being is popularly expressed in the Zen maxim *byojo shin, kore michi nari*, or "ordinary mind is the Way." Most people don't realize it, but these words belong to Mazu Daoyi.

2

Keep Yourself Unstained

"There's no need to trouble yourself with mastering the Way. It's enough if you just take care to keep yourself unstained. We become stained by being overindulgent in life, fearing death, striving, and chasing after goals. If you want to grasp the Way directly, it is none other than your ordinary mind."

道不用修。但莫污染。何為污染。但有生死心、造作趨向、皆是污染。若欲直會其道、平常心是道。

If you turn the Way into an object to be grasped, into a goal or a thing to be sought for, you end up having the opposite effect: contaminating the Way. So how do we keep from setting goals and seeking? "In whatever you do, just live ordinary life," says Mazu.

So does this mean we can take "ordinary mind is the Way" at face value and just piddle on with our daily life? Not quite. That amounts to no more than a lazy sort of self-satisfaction.

The saying "ordinary mind is the Way" owes its fame to Mazu, but it is almost equally famous for its appearance in a dialogue that takes place between Nanquan, a disciple of Mazu, and his disciple Zhaozhou:

Zhaozhou asked Nanquan, "Just what is the Way?"

"It's your ordinary mind."

"So that's what one should aim for?"

"Aiming for it only puts it further away."

"Without aiming for it, how can you know the Way?"

"The Way has nothing to do with knowing and not-knowing. To say that you know it would be error; to say that you don't would just show indifference. When you truly attain the Way of no-aims, everything clears up like the cloudless, empty sky. There's no need to scrutinize everything for right and wrong."

Zhaozhou immediately awakened to the most profound truth, and his heart shone like the clear, bright moon.

When Zhaozhou asks, "What is the Way?" he is concerned only with the goal of enlightenment, seeing the process leading up to it as secondary. So Nanquan admonishes him: "Your ordinary way of being is itself the Way." In the Zen school, the act of walking itself is more important than arriving at the destination. Moreover, the experience of seeing plants and wildflowers along the road and listening to the birds' voices floating in the air is enjoyable, too, Mazu says.

Zhaozhou's objection to the ordinary being the Way is something like this: "That may be so, but you can't walk without having the will to walk." In other words, it's all well and good to enjoy things along the way, but no one just starts walking without first deciding to do so.

"Hang on," says Nanquan. "You don't need to make such a big deal of it, this business of 'making decisions' just to go out for a stroll. If you have to grit your teeth and say, 'Okay. *Now I will put one foot in front of the other and in so doing go over there*,' or fix your gaze on a certain point ahead saying, 'Right. *Just a little further*,' it stops being simply walking."

Zhaozhou still insists, "If you don't know where you're going, how do you even start walking? It's not like we're sleepwalking, recklessly stumbling about."

But, according to Nanquan, when you find yourself unable to abide in your ordinary mind—if you start striving and making all kinds of effort to get back to it— you end up losing it even further. *Trying* to "abide in your ordinary mind" is not abiding in your ordinary mind.

Zhaozhou still refuses to give up. "If that's the case, then ordinary mind being the Way loses all its meaning." Here Zhaozhou's complaint actually makes some sense. A path, a way, is something that you can stray from; it is also something that you can return to. There must be something that can objectively be called "the Way." To Zhaozhou, "ordinary mind" doesn't seem to satisfy these conditions.

The rather serious Zhaozhou sees things as being related in terms of means and ends. If you think in those terms, anything that doesn't fit into the means-ends relationship becomes incomprehensible, meaningless, and useless. Is zazen really nothing but a means to attain enlightenment? If you don't get enlightened, does that mean that sitting zazen was without meaning?

Nanquan rejects that way of thinking outright: it's not about knowing that "This is the Way" or "This is not the Way." And zazen is the same: sitting zazen is not about becoming enlightened or not becoming enlightened. The act of sitting has value in and of itself. Yet even saying that something "has value" can be misleading. Rather, let's just say that if you sit zazen as a "Way of no-aims," at some point your way of being will become enlightenment.

Ordinary mind *is* the Way, no question. That's why it is delusion to "aim for" ordinary mind. Still, to specifically aim for nothing whatsoever shows a lack of concern. "You should continually walk by the Way of no-aims," says Nanquan. And apparently, that did it for Zhaozhou.

Let's suppose for a moment that the opposite of ordinary mind is "being irritated." We might imagine Zen means that, however irritating your situation may be, you must absolutely not get irritated. We could take this further, imagining that Zen requires that not only must you avoid mood swings, you must practically avoid everything emotional. This is not what we mean by "ordinary mind." To be irritated when you are in an irritating situation is perfectly human. This moving, swaying heart-mind is our true way of being. Accept it, says Nanquan.

If you tell yourself that you must not get irritated, it only serves to increase your irritation. Try instead to just good-naturedly accept yourself as you are: "Ah. Looks like I'm irritated, right now." What's important is whether you can do that or not.

Even if you've thoroughly grasped that your ordinary mind is the Way, it doesn't mean that you're not going to get irritated anymore. And if you can accept your irritated self, it will probably make things a whole lot easier.

3

On a Beautiful Moonlit Evening

One evening Mazu was enjoying the beauty of the moon along with his disciples Xitang Zhizang, Baizhang Huaihai, and Nanquan Puyuan. Mazu asked, "What should we do on such a nice evening as this?"

Xitang replied, "It's perfect for reading sutras."

"It's perfect for practicing zazen," said Baizhang.

Nanquan shook his sleeves and walked away.

Mazu commented: "Sutras go in the storehouse, and Zen returns to the sea. [Nanquan] Puyuan alone transcends the material world."

西堂、百丈、南泉、侍祖翫月次、祖曰、正恁麼時如何。西堂云、正好供養。百丈云、正好修行。南泉払袖便去。祖云、経入蔵、禅帰海。唯有普願独超物外。

Mazu's three disciples all show some degree of excellence, but their individuality shows through as well. Each has his own unique answer to Mazu's question, "What should we do on such a nice evening as this?" Xitang says it's good for reading scriptures and dedicating their merit. Baizhang suggests it's a good time to sit zazen. Nanquan just walks away.

In Mazu's comment, he is, in part, playing on the first two disciples' names. Xitang Zhizang's name contains the character for "storehouse" (蔵, zang), and Baizhang Huaihai's name contains the character for "sea" (海, hai). Essentially, Mazu is invoking the storehouse of Dharma teachings in reference to one student and vast oceanic depths of Zen practice in reference to another. Nanquan, though, in Mazu's estimation, is beyond metaphor. Puns aside, Mazu is basically saying, "Xitang excels at theory, and Baizhang excels at practice, but Nanquan is beyond them both." So tell me this, does this mean that he considers Nanquan to be a special case?

Xitang devotes his energies to mastering his mind, and Baizhang devotes himself to mastering his body, and Nanquan is beyond getting caught up with mind or body. Xitang goes off to the sutra house to study, and Baizhang goes off to the meditation hall to sit zazen, but it looks like Nanquan just took off and soared through the sky to the moon. Indeed, it does seem that Nanquan is a special case.

The studier keeps on studying regardless of whether it's going to rain or snow. The zazen-sitter always sits zazen, regardless of whether it looks like it's going to be windy or stormy. Neither of them tries to get outside of their own little world. "Seeing as how the moon is shining so elegantly this evening, why not enjoy it?" says Nanquan. "If you can't come and enjoy it with me, I'll just go by myself."

I think we have to go ahead and declare Nanquan the winner this time.

4

Lift High Your Eyes!

Layman Pang said to Mazu: "As an original man beyond delusion, I ask you: lift high your eyes!"

Mazu looked straight down.

"None but you, Master, can so skillfully play the stringless harp!"

Mazu looked straight up.

Pang bowed reverently.

Mazu went back to his quarters.

Pang followed. "I thought I'd show off my skill, but instead I only blundered."

問祖云、不昧本来人、請師高著眼。祖直下覷。士云、一種沒絃琴、唯師弾得妙。師直上覷。士乃作礼。祖帰方丈。士随後入曰、適来弄巧成拙。

Let's consider a rather straightforward reading of this dialogue. Told to look up, Mazu instead looks down.

When praised, he ignores the praise and looks straight up. Pang realizes that he mistook Mazu for someone he could go up against.

Layman Pang knows himself as an "original man": 本来人, a man of the highest ideal, who never wavers. Still, he's troubled that perhaps even an original man can be of a higher or lesser quality than another. So he asks Mazu to demonstrate for him what a first-class original man looks like. "Don't just look down from above as a teacher; let me see you set your sights even higher!"

Mazu deliberately looks down. An original man has no high and low; he neither improves nor backslides. Pang assents and then continues with the image of the stringless harp: this perfection with no upper limits, is it not like a harp without strings?

Mazu looks straight up. There's always someone better. Do away with playing, but *play*: this is the stringless harp.

In the beginning, Pang dramatically declares, "As an original man beyond delusion, I ask you . . ." Perhaps he asks his question "as an original man" in order to provoke Mazu: "*I'm* an original man, but what about *you?*" Impressive vigor, but he's far too excited. Again, his "lift your eyes high!" is a challenge to Mazu; if he truly is an original man, he ought to show some evidence. These are fighting words.

But if you do happen to be an original person, you don't concern yourself with high and low. Mazu looks straight down, putting a damper on Pang's enthusiasm.

Layman Pang then praises him: "Only you, Master, can play the stringless harp so well." There's a bit of pride hidden within his flattering statement. It looks as though Pang is complementing Mazu, but he is actually insinuating that he, too, knows a thing or two about how to play the stringless harp.

Dumping a bucket of cold water on Pang's vanity, Mazu looks straight up, as if to say, "Are you still pressing on with this nonsense?"

Mazu is not just messing around with Pang; his looking up, looking down, and so on is actually quite sincere. When Mazu walks away, Layman Pang appropriately concludes by hanging his head.

But what if Pang's "original man" refers to Mazu? Pang, then, would be asking him to show concretely what it looks like to unwaveringly hold to only the highest ideal. How does an original man live? What does it look like?

Mazu shows him by looking down; it's not only about looking up. Sometimes you have to look down, too. You can't just drown yourself in ideals; you have to remember the reality that's right here at your feet.

Pang doesn't flinch, even after Mazu looks straight down at him. He wants to celebrate him as an original man no matter what: "None but you, Master, can so skillfully play the stringless harp!"

And Mazu looks straight up. "You think I'm perfect? If you concern yourself with who's 'superior' and who's not, there's always going to be someone better than you."

5

How Natural

Zen Master Danxia Tianran visited Mazu. Without so much as a greeting, he entered the meditation hall and sat astride the neck of a bodhisattva statue. Astonished, the monks nearby informed Mazu immediately.

Mazu proceeded to the meditation hall, and seeing for himself, said: "My own disciple! How natural!"

Danxia came down, bowed reverently, and said: "Thank you for granting me such a splendid Dharma name." Thus he took on the name Tianran.

丹霞天然禅師、再参祖。未参礼便入僧堂内、騎聖僧頸而坐。時大衆驚愕、遽報祖。祖躬入堂視之日、我子天然。霞即下地礼拝日、謝師賜法号。因名天然。

The word *Tianran* (天然), which above is translated as "natural," refers to childlike innocence; someone who has nothing hidden, whose true self shows through just as it is. Personally, I wonder if Danxia is really being so "natural." His behavior reeks of fake-natural. In the world of Zen, replete with formal customs and practices, one doesn't just strike an off-the-wall pose for no reason.

Climbing up the bodhisattva statue and sitting astride its neck like he does, Danxia is trying to provoke Mazu into scolding him. He's running a campaign against himself.

Danxia is a hot-blooded man; it doesn't suit his nature to go about acting the well-mannered part of a Zen priest. Putting on a serious face like he's been enlightened and acting as an example for the masses would be too confining. Wanting to get himself out of his oppressive situation, he deliberately makes a show of his misconduct. "Hurry up and brand me a miscreant so I can relax, okay?"

But Mazu isn't going to let him off the hook so easily. Just as he thinks he's about to receive a severe upbraiding ("This is an outrage!"), he instead gets thrown a lifeline: "How splendidly childlike!"

Mazu turns out to be an even better actor than Danxia, who, left with no other hand to play, says, "Fine. From here on out, I'm an officially licensed 'natural.' And since I have my master's seal of approval, I'll just keep on acting naturally right through to the end."

Mazu looks at the heart, rather than the surface of things. Danxia is looking for a scolding, but Mazu responds to what's truly going on inside of him instead of reacting to what appears on the surface.

6

To Give Up Your Life

Baizhang asked Mazu, "What is the essential meaning of Buddhism?"

"To give up your life."

百丈問、如何是仏旨趣。祖云、正是汝放身命処。

One scholar translates Mazu's answer as "Truly, it's where you give up your life." This would mean "As soon as you grasp the essence, you'll give up your life" or "If you're ready to give up your life, I'll tell you about the Buddha's essence." If you talk to your disciples so threateningly, they're just going to shrink back in fear, right?

I hear it differently. Baizhang asks, "What is the essential meaning of Buddhism?"

And Mazu replies, "If you just live for all you're worth, you're doing fine."

Baizhang, like a child holding a sharpened blade, all of a sudden comes at Mazu brandishing a ridiculously lofty question—and Mazu calms him down, telling him he doesn't need to go around worrying about such things.

If to know the essential meaning of Buddhism were literally to give up your life, timid folks such as myself would quit our practice just like that. I don't think that Mazu is being so threatening. I think he's speaking gently, with a laugh: "If you want to know the essential meaning of Buddhism, so long as you have life for the present, all you can do is continue your practice, right?"

Of course, though we're not generally aware of it, the truth is that to live is to have your life constantly hanging in the balance, in eating, in sleeping, in walking—in all of the acts of our daily lives. The phrase "your life" in Mazu's reply refers to that which is always in the balance: you, your way of being. The "give up" part refers to giving up being particular about your self. "Don't cling to yourself, your way of being," says Mazu. "Your life is constantly in the balance, but don't worry about that; just keep on living here, living now."

7

Sudden!

One day, while with Mazu, Master Magu Baoche said, "What is the Great Nirvana like?"

"Sudden!"

"Just what is 'sudden'?"

"Look at water!"

麻谷宝徹禅師、一日随祖行次問、如何是大涅槃。祖云、急。徹云、急箇什麼。祖云、看水。

Master Magu begins with a bit of an over-the-top question. It's the Great Nirvana. Since you entered the world by birth, your death is inevitable. No matter how much you don't want to die, you still will at some point. The time of your death is growing nearer moment by moment. For each day you live, your death draws one day closer. For each second you live, your death draws one second closer. This is truly a matter of the greatest importance.

It feels as though Mazu's "Sudden!" means that the Great Nirvana is no subject for casual questions. "'What's the Great Nirvana?' Do you know what you're getting into?" If this is the case, then Mazu's reply is not the result of a cool-headed analysis: "Why, it is 'sudden.'" Maybe it's more of a full-bodied reaction: "Look out!"

Even after Mazu's direct response, he gets another head-in-the-clouds question from Magu: "And just what is 'sudden'?" In response, Mazu tells him to look at water.

Some waters take their time; others flow by swiftly. In either case, they are flowing moment by moment; whether the flow is fast or slow in the moment is a separate issue. The moment that flows into nirvana—that moment's *suddenness*—is most certainly what Mazu wants to teach. The character rendered "sudden" (急) in its absolute sense means "moment," as well as a range of other nuanced meanings including "to hurry" and "to prepare oneself." Water is constantly flowing. However, if you look at a fixed point, in a moment the water flows up to you, and in a moment it flows away. This flow is the same at any given moment, regardless of how fast the river is flowing. That moment is eternity, nirvana. It defies any attempt at human control. This is the moment to which Mazu is calling our attention.

That's my understanding of it, anyway. Another scholar translates "look at water" as "that water over there." We tend to just trot along at some arbitrary rhythm, but we don't know when nirvana is going to come. We should practice constantly, without letting our attention wander, like the unceasing flow of the stream. Confucius said, "Thus is that which passes, resting neither day nor night." Perhaps Mazu, too, means "It's like that water right before your eyes, flowing constantly and without rest." Your practice, that which leads to nirvana, is the same—don't slack off, don't miss it!

When Mazu says to look at water, I think he's admonishing us to give proper, unceasing attention to this moment, here and now. Look at the unceasing moment, says Mazu. It's nirvana. Only because it is "sudden" can we call it nirvana.

8

Tending Cattle

One day, Mazu asked one of the monks working in the kitchen, "What are you doing?"

"Tending cattle."

"And how do you tend them?"

"When they stray into the grass, I pull them back by the nose."

"A true cowherd, indeed."

一日在廚作務次、祖問曰、作什麼。曰、牧牛。祖曰、作麼生牧。曰、一迴入草去、便把鼻孔拽来。祖曰、子真牧牛。

You lead the cattle out into the pasture to let them graze. Once there, the cattle are quite excited and graze happily. It's not good for them, though, to eat too much. Once they've had enough, you grab their noses out of the thick grass to keep them from over-indulging their appetites.

Water flows toward lower ground; the ability to regulate this flow is key to farming. Cows' appetites are similar to water. There's no need to teach them how to follow their cravings; let them go free and they'll still seek to satisfy them. Even though it looks like they still want to eat more, you have to give them some "tough love" and pull them out of the grass by the nose. They protest—"I was still eating!! Mooooo!"—but soon give up, reluctantly. Taking good care of the cows—even when they don't want you to—is part of the cowherd's job.

The next passage is from *The Record of Linji*.

Entering the kitchen, Huangbo asked the monk in charge of cooking the rice, "What are you doing?"

"I'm picking the little bits of dirt out of the rice we're going to feed everyone."

"How much do we eat in a day?"

"About 400 kilograms."

"Isn't that too much?"

"I'm afraid it might not be enough."

Huangbo immediately hit him.

The cook later told Linji about what had happened.

"I'll go see what's up with the old man for you," said Linji, who then went to see Huangbo, who related to him what had happened with the cook.

Linji said, "The cook doesn't get it. Master, how about a word to wake him up?" And then Linji asked Huangbo, "Isn't that too much?"

Huangbo replied, "Why not say, 'We'll eat again tomorrow'?"

"Why talk about tomorrow? Eat it now!" said Linji and gave Huangbo a slap.

"This crazy fool, coming to pull the tiger's whiskers again!" said Huangbo.

Linji gave a shout and exited.

Looks like the cook gave the wrong answer. So the cook goes and complains to Linji, who in turn asks Huangbo to reveal the correct answer. "If there's any left over, we can just eat it tomorrow," answers Huangbo—but Linji puts a big red X over that answer, too. "Eat what's there when it's there. Don't talk about tomorrow, eat it now!" Smack!

Huangbo is emphasizing the need to control one's desires. For Huangbo, there's no need to worry about not having enough, and if there's some extra, the important thing is to curb your appetite.

But Linji takes a different tack. "Don't worry about too much or too little. When there's food, eat it. When there's not, don't. That's all," he says. "Don't bring tomorrow into the equation at all."

It certainly seems that Linji gets the upper hand here, but if we consider that, in practice, maintaining a religious order necessitates that one deal with rice rations efficiently, then we have room to sympathize with Huangbo as well. I'm sure there are many worries that you can't understand until you meet certain circumstances. Granted, these are mere worldly problems.

The cook is concerned with satisfying the monks' desires for ample rice, but monks shouldn't eat just because they want to. That would serve only to enslave them to their appetites.

Comparing human desires to tending cattle, Mazu says, "Tame your desires." When monks are about to poke their noses into the grassy field of worldly desires, their teacher may grab them and pull them out—"Come on, now." With cattle, this is of course the cowherd's job. But when monks are about to be defeated by their desires, overprotecting them with a "Come on, now!" and pulling them out will inevitably become a hindrance to their practice. One must, I suppose, be responsible for one's self. When Mazu says, "A true cowherd, indeed," I suspect he doesn't mean it as a compliment.

9

Is the Lake Full?

Mazu asked a monk, "Where did you come from?"

"I came from Hunan."

"Is the East Lake full?"

"No."

"All that rain, and it's still not full?"

祖問僧、什麼処来。云、湖南来。祖云、東湖水満也未。云、未。祖云、許多時雨、水尚未満。

Perhaps the monk says "no" because he's taking Mazu's question plainly, at face value, answering according to the actual volume of water in the East Lake. "Nope, it's not at its full capacity just yet." He is pleasantly innocent but kind of blockheaded.

But it seems that the monk came from Hunan, where Master Nanyue Huairang taught. When Mazu asks the monk if the East Lake is full of water, he's asking him if he's had all the teaching he needs: "Seeing as you've been practicing under the likes of Master Huairang, you must feel quite fulfilled, yes?" So when the monk says no, one interpretation is that the monk cannot with confidence tell Mazu yes, because he doesn't fully believe that he already has all that he needs. Mazu's answer is an expression of his amazement that even though the monk had all that welcome rain showered on him from Huairang, he still feels himself to be lacking.

Mazu might have further replied, "But it must be full by now . . . perhaps you just don't realize it." The monk already has all he could ever need. He doesn't lack a thing.

It's not that Zen practitioners don't ever speak plainly, but Mazu doesn't just spit out superficial words. In this case, Mazu isn't literally asking about the lake's water level; he's greeting the monk with a witty question— "How's your practice?"

When someone greets you, you respond appropriately. If it's a nice day and someone greets you with "Nice weather, huh?" you probably don't say "nope" and let the conversation die flat. You likely agree and continue the conversation from there. The same applies in the Zen world. When a Zen master greets you with a slightly poetic question about your practice, you respond appropriately. The monk ought to have known the nature of the question here.

And perhaps he did. It is, of course, possible that the two understand each other perfectly and just carry on with each other playfully. Even so, this is the question Mazu wants to communicate: "You're already a buddha, and you're still saying you're lacking?"

Part II

Don't Just Sit There!

10

Whip the Cart, or Whip the Ox?

During the beginning of the Tang dynasty, while Mazu was practicing at Hengyue's Chuan Fayuan temple, he met Master Huairang.

Perceiving that Mazu was an able vessel for carrying on his Dharma, Huairang asked him, "Virtuous monk, what do you intend to accomplish by sitting zazen?"

"I intend to become a buddha."

Huairang then proceeded to take a tile and began polishing it in view of Mazu.

"Why are you polishing that tile?" asked Mazu.

"I'm going to polish it into a mirror."

"Polishing a tile won't ever make it into a mirror."

"Just as polishing won't make a tile into a mirror, sitting zazen will never make you into a buddha."

"Then what should I do?"

"If you hitch an ox to a cart and the cart doesn't move, do you whip the cart or the ox?"

Mazu was lost for words.

唐開元中、習定於衡嶽伝法院、遇讓和尚。知是法器、問曰、大德、坐禅図什麼。師曰、図作仏。讓乃取一磚、於彼菴前磨。師曰、磨磚作麼。讓曰、磨作鏡。師曰、磨磚豈得成鏡。讓曰、磨磚既不成鏡、坐禅豈得成仏耶。師曰、如何即是。讓曰、如牛駕車車不行、打車即是、打牛即是。師無対。

Mazu knows that you can't polish a tile into a mirror, but he thinks that he can sit himself into a buddha. Like a dog that only knows a single trick, Mazu sits zazen with reckless single-mindedness.

Huairang perceives that Mazu has potential and considers it a shame to let it go to waste, so he lets Mazu know he's off-track: "That's not going to get you any-where. If you think you can become a buddha just by sitting zazen, you're making a big mistake." Concerned about the inflexibility that he sees in Mazu, Huairang tells Mazu that there's no need to treat zazen like it's everything.

Even so, is Huairang's tile metaphor really hitting the mark? Right, so you can't polish a tile into a mir-ror. But is it really the same for humans—no amount of sitting will make you into a buddha? Is sitting zazen therefore just a waste of effort?

When no matter how much you polish a tile it still won't become a mirror, blaming the tile isn't going to get you anywhere. But if you're still bent on making a mirror out of it, then there's nothing left to do but continue to polish it diligently, ad infinitum. When no matter how much you sit you still don't become a buddha, blaming yourself isn't going to do anything, either. And if you're still determined to become a buddha, then there's nothing to do but just keep on sitting.

There is no necessary connection between zazen (practice) and attaining buddhahood (enlightenment). Zazen itself is the expression of buddhahood.

Huairang then hits Mazu with another question: "Do you whip the cart or the ox?"

You hitch an ox to your cart, but it doesn't move. If you whip the cart, it's not going to accomplish anything. Maybe it's the same with zazen. If you're just trying to endure the pain in your legs, you won't get anywhere; it's your mind that you have to work on, i.e., the ox and not the cart.

Even so, it's not just a simple matter of "whip the ox and everything's okay." If we keep on with a dualistic way of thinking, separating mind and body, we're just going to get further and further away from enlightenment. If the ox moves, so does the cart. The cart is built to be able to move, and of course so is the ox. To say at a certain time that it's not moving is to imply that, at the proper time, it will move. Your body is made so that it can sit, and your mind is made so that it can be enlightened.

Zazen is the "you" who is to be enlightened, sitting; the "you" that is already a buddha is sitting.

Of course, even though you're already a buddha, it's surprisingly difficult to think of yourself that way. You get more and more stiff as you sit. This is where Huairang would say, "Easy, there. No need to get so uptight."

Since we use the phrase "attaining buddhahood," the problem of "becoming a buddha" is bound to arise. However, you already *are* a buddha. The key lies in whether or not you sit with that understanding. If you use sitting zazen as a means to *become* a buddha, it won't happen—no matter how long you sit.

Zazen from the start is sitting-buddha; there is no question of the self "becoming" a buddha. To think that you can sit yourself into a buddha is like trying to polish a tile into a mirror. If you whip the ox with the idea that you're going to make him move, with the instrumental mentality of means and ends, he won't move at all.

So, without any whipping, you just clamber up into the cart—but this isn't going to get you anywhere, either. If whipping the ox doesn't get you anywhere, why not try being gentle with him now and then?

When no amount of sitting will make you into a buddha, sitting with a goal in mind is not going to solve your problem either. The key is to change your way of being, to sit as the "you" who is a buddha.

Speaking of "being," the difference between that and "doing" bears mentioning.

Alive as we are, "being" without some sort of "doing"—speaking, eating, etc.—simply doesn't happen. In fact, to be consciously aware of your "being,"

you have to turn it into a mental abstraction; aware-
ness of being takes some extra work. Perhaps for that
reason, living in this world wherein one brings about
changes in things that *are* by *doing* something, we tend
to put more value on the doing. Still, I don't think it's
right to make light of *being*.

In educational institutions, *doing* is generally val-
ued over *being*. Still, when it comes to *being* a student
(a way of being that applies equally to everyone) and
the work of *doing* your studies, both the *being* and the
doing are indispensable, right? Many students, especially elementary school students, are not yet independent adults; it would seem that cultivating their sense
of *being*—their sense of seeing with their own eyes
and standing on their own feet—would be of primary
importance. Their *doing*—learning math drills, memo-
rizing vocabulary—must be acknowledged as things
that are made possible by their *being*. When Huairang
sets to polishing a tile in front of Mazu, perhaps he is
teaching that *becoming* a buddha is only made possible
by *being* yourself.

However, your *being* (your self), in its current
state, is like the Buddha only in your *being* of like
kind. If, merely being of like kind with the Buddha,
you are as of yet incomplete and imperfect, for that
very reason you need to seek fullness and perfection
through your practice. When Huairang continues with
"Do you whip the cart or the ox?" he is suggesting that
doing—that is, the act of expressing one's self through
sitting—is what allows you to *be* a buddha.

11

Who's Sitting, and Why?

Huairang said, "Do you sit to learn Zen? Do you sit as a buddha? If you sit to learn Zen, Zen does not equal sitting. If you sit as a buddha, buddha is not a fixed posture. In the nonabiding Dharma, you can't go about discriminating like that. If you simply 'sit as a buddha,' you kill the Buddha. If you get attached to the form of sitting, you will never arrive at truth."

Mazu heard these teachings and drank them in like sweet nectar.

讓又曰、汝為学坐禅、為学坐仏。若学坐禅、禅非坐臥。若学坐仏、仏非定相。於無住法、不応取捨。汝若坐仏、即是殺仏。若執坐相、非達其理。師聞示誨、如飲醍醐。

Starting out by learning a certain form such as sitting and watching your breath can often be quite effective at settling the mind. However, even if learning an external form is what got you started on the path of meditation, once you get attached to forms (i.e., zazen), you are no longer practicing Zen.

Huairang asks, "Do you sit to learn Zen? Do you sit as a buddha?" If zazen does not consist of sitting as a buddha, it becomes nothing but a mere form. To become attached to form is to kill the Buddha. Sitting by itself does not comprise Zen. Sitting becomes Zen only when it can be called "sitting Buddha." Only when you start sitting as your true self, who already is a buddha, does sitting become Zen.

Unless you sit as a buddha, it's not zazen. But Buddha does not have a fixed form; in what way should we sit so as to "sit as a buddha"? Not an easy question to answer. Offering another hurdle, Huairang teaches that to merely "sit as a buddha" is to kill the Buddha. It's not enough simply to avoid getting caught up in forms and postures; you also have to avoid getting attached to the idea that you are already a buddha.

The one who does the sitting is your self; your self is the one who is sitting as a buddha. "Sitting Buddha" does not mean that, through the act of sitting, your self becomes a buddha. Rather, it means that in your sitting self—Buddha, as Buddha—is manifest.

Self is self, and Buddha is Buddha. The two are not immediately identical. They are not one and the same, but they are not separate, either. Self and Buddha are not-two. Sitting Zen is sitting Zen, and sitting Buddha is sitting Buddha, but they are not-two.

When the one sitting zazen is your true self, the statement "sitting as a buddha" applies. The self never "becomes" a buddha, nor does zazen "become" sitting-Buddha. As soon as you start thinking in terms of one thing "becoming" another thing, you kill the Buddha. Self and Buddha are not-two.

Neglecting the self and making sitting out to be everything will never amount to "sitting as a buddha." Huairang is simply criticizing getting overly attached to zazen, with its specific forms; he's not some sort of anti-zazen crusader. He just wanted to make sure that Mazu didn't think that all he had to do was sit.

Let's take a closer look at what it means that self and Buddha are not identical yet not separate, through a dialogue from *The Record of Linji*:

A lecture master came to visit Linji.

Linji asked, "What sutras do you lecture on?"

"Not enough, I suppose. I have a rough grasp of the Treatise on the Hundred Dharmas."

Linji said, "One person has mastered all the sutras; another person has mastered none. Are they the same, or are they different?"

"If you've mastered the sutras, then they're the same. If you haven't, then they're different."

Linji's attendant Lepu said from behind him, "Lecture Master, just where do you think you are, talking about 'same' and 'different'?"

Linji spun around and asked him, "What about you?"

Lepu let out a shout.

Linji saw the lecture master off, then came back and asked Lepu, "That shout back there, was that for me?"

"That's right."

Linji hit him.

Asked by Linji what sutras he's studying, the lecture master modestly replies, implying that he is not at all advanced, that he was just trying to work his way through the Treatise on the Hundred Dharmas. Having been approached so humbly, Linji won't be dealing out any blows.

Linji asks further, "One person has mastered all the sutras; another person has mastered none"—which is better? Which is closer to enlightenment: a university-graduate scholar-monk, or an uneducated wandering monk?

In Buddhism, we find the proposition that "All sentient beings have buddha nature." If so, those who read sutras and those who do not read sutras are both on equal ground. Thus, the lecture master replies that those who have understood the truth would discern that everyone is equal since all sentient beings have buddha nature, and that those whose practice is insufficient would probably still hold various biases and discriminations. A perfectly common-sense reply.

Lepu chimes in from nearby. "What are you talking about with this same/different nonsense?" Maybe the lecture master's common-sense answer irritated him. Or is he trying to say that sutras basically don't matter? Linji says, "What about you?" and Lepu snaps back with a shout, probably saying that whether or not you can understand sutras has nothing to do with enlightenment. This in itself is perfectly fine. But now it turns into an exchange between master and disciple.

Linji sees the lecture master off and asks Lepu, "That shout back there—was that for me?" "That's right," comes Lepu's cold reply, and Lepu has thus taken Linji's bait. It's fine to shout at a lecture master, but directing it to your teacher is off base.

Those who can understand sutras and those who can't are different. Some differences we just have to accept as they are. For example, dogs and people are different.

The way one interacts with the lecture master, who can't understand the sutras, is different from the way one should interact with Linji, who does understand them.

The lecture master says that those who understand the sutras realize that all students of the sutras are the same, but those who do not understand think that some are different. Lepu suggests that the lecture master is missing the meaning of "same" because those who understand sutras are actually on the same ground as those who don't understand sutras. Different and same are not-two.

Some understand, and some do not—but those who understand are equal to those who don't.

12

Messing with a Zazen Zealot

One day Master Weijian of Letan was sitting zazen behind the Dharma hall. Seeing him there, Mazu blew in his ears twice. Weijian came out of his meditation, saw that it was Mazu, and went right back into meditation. Mazu returned to his quarters and had his attendant bring Weijian a cup of tea. Weijian went back into the Dharma hall without giving it so much as a glance.

泐潭惟建禅師、一日在法堂後坐禅。祖見之乃吹建耳両吹。建起定、見是祖、却復入定。祖帰方丈、令侍者持一椀茶与建。建不顧、便自帰堂。

Weijian takes his practice very seriously. Blowing in his ears, Mazu says, "You're sitting zazen not only inside the Dharma hall, but behind it as well? Such a hard worker!" Mazu's feeling is understandable; when you see someone taking themselves so seriously, it makes you want to mess with them, to do something to lighten them up a little.

The catch is that he was sitting zazen *behind* the Dharma hall. Why does he have to do it there? What's wrong with sitting inside? It's like he's sneaking around with some kind of ulterior motive; maybe he wants to get the edge on everyone else and out-sit them. If he had been sitting inside the Dharma hall, Mazu may not have tried to mess with him.

Mazu blows in his ears: "Quit practicing in shady places like this and go into the Dharma hall—that's what it's there for." Weijian doesn't care to listen. So, Mazu has his attendant bring him some tea, suggesting he can't just sit all the time. Why not have some tea? Mazu is trying to get Weijian to relax a little and stop taking himself so seriously. Weijian, not even acknowledging the tea, gets up and hurries back inside the Dharma hall, where he resumes his practice.

Recall the story about when Mazu was sitting absorbed in zazen and Huairang started polishing a tile in front of him. "It's not just about sitting." This is not so different from Mazu having tea brought to Weijian. "You're absorbed in Zen—good Buddha. Have some tea. By the way, zazen doesn't work when you get so uptight about it."

Weijian, having his practice interrupted, isn't willing to play along with Mazu. Annoyed and wishing to be left alone, Weijan moves to the Dharma hall and seems to say, "Sure, Zen's not just about sitting, but I can still sit if I want to."

13

Damned If You Do, Damned If You Don't: So What Do You Do?

It was Master Weiyan of Yaoshan's first visit to Shitou. He asked, "I'm basically familiar with the scriptures, but I still can't seem to understand the southern teachings of 'point directly to the mind' and 'see one's nature and attain buddhahood.' Master, would you please have compassion and show me their meaning?"

Shitou replied: "You can't do, you can't not-do, and you can't neither-do-nor-not-do. What do you do?"

Yaoshan didn't know what to say.

Shitou said, "This isn't the right place for you. Why don't you go and see Master Mazu?"

Yaoshan went to see Mazu as he had been told. After greeting him reverently, he asked Mazu the same question.

Mazu replied, "There is a time to blink, and a time not to blink. There is a time for a certain one to blink, and a time for the same one not to blink. What do you do?"

Upon hearing these words, Yaoshan was enlightened and immediately bowed reverently.

Mazu asked, "What truth did you see to make you bow?"

"At Shitou's place, I was like a mosquito on an iron bull."

"If that's how it is, take good care of yourself."

薬山惟儼禅師、初参石頭便問、三乗十二分教、某甲粗知。常聞南方直指人心、見性成　仏、実未明了。伏望和尚慈悲指示。頭曰、恁麼也不得、不恁麼也不得、恁麼不恁麼総不得、子作麼生。山罔措。頭曰、子因縁不在此。且往馬大師処去。山稟命恭礼祖、仍伸前問。祖曰、我有時教伊揚眉瞬目、有時不教伊揚眉瞬目、有時揚眉瞬目者是、有時揚眉瞬目者不是、子作麼生。山於言下契悟、便礼拝。祖曰、你見甚麼道理便礼拝。山曰、某甲在石頭処、如蚊子上鉄牛。祖曰、汝既如是、善自護持。

Shitou says that you can't affirm reality, can't deny reality, and can't get away with doing neither of the two, and then comes at Yaoshan with "What do you do?" Shitou's line may be taken as a challenge: "How do you apprehend something that can be described neither positively nor negatively using words?"

The teaching to abandon all forms of discrimination is correct. However, it's not realistic. Thus, realistically speaking, it's not correct. There may not be a single "right" way of doing things, but doing nothing at all doesn't work either.

Mazu takes a more flexible perspective on reality. "It's not that there is nothing finite whatsoever. Sometimes things simply are, and one thing might be more appropriate than another, and you have to decide between this and that. That's important, too."

Shitou and Mazu are not teaching different things here. They are teaching the not-two-ness of reality, which means that two things are at once "like" but also "not like." It's just that since Shitou is putting it in completely absolute terms, there's no way to wrap your head around it. Mazu, on the other hand, always teaches in terms of dealing with the reality that exists here and now, in terms of blinking, for example, which tends to be a bit more encouraging for his students.

We get overly concerned about things like having money and not having money. Mazu's "There's a time to blink, and a time not to blink" tells us that when we have money, we can eat sushi; when we don't, we can eat instant ramen. The idea is to free yourself from worrying about limitations, whether of money, time, or anything else.

However, if you say "to hell with money" and throw it away in the sewer, you're actually still acting quite concerned with money. If you must throw your money away, at least make sure you throw away your concern along with it.

It appears that Yaoshan was enlightened upon hearing Mazu's teaching. He proceeds to complain that "being with Shitou was like being a mosquito sitting on an iron bull." He wanted to suck a little blood but couldn't get even a drop. At that, Mazu leaves him to himself: "If that's the case, do it yourself from here on."

So is Mazu's teaching style really any gentler than Shitou's? Somehow I don't think so. Shitou's method is definitely too tough for Yaoshan; an iron bull doesn't care whether or not a mosquito lands on it. But when Shitou passes him on to the seemingly more patient Mazu, it still ends up in a "Well, do as you like, then." Mazu doesn't turn out to be so gentle, either.

14

What Are You Seeking?

It was Master Huilang of Tanzhou's first visit to Mazu.

Mazu asked, "What do you seek in coming here?"

"I seek the Buddha's knowledge."

Mazu said, "The Buddha has no knowledge. Knowledge is for demons. Where did you come from?"

"From Nanyue."

"You came from Nanyue, and you still haven't realized the heart of the Sixth Patriarch's Zen? You'd better get right back to Nanyue. It's not good to go grazing in other pastures."

潭州慧朗禅師、初参祖。祖問、汝来何求。曰、求仏知見。祖曰、仏無知見。知見乃魔耳。汝自何来。曰、南岳来。曰、汝従南岳来、未識曹溪心要。汝速帰彼、不宜他往。

Nanyue Huairang is the link between Mazu and the Sixth Patriarch Huineng; Huineng was Huairang's teacher, and Huairang was Mazu's, as well as Huilang's. So Huilang comes from a good dojo, one connected directly to Zen's backbone—yet he still doesn't quite get it.

This reminds me of the episode where Mazu meets Huairang, when asked, "What do you hope to accomplish by sitting zazen?" "I want to become a buddha," replied Mazu, and Huairang started polishing a tile. Still, the young Mazu didn't beat around the bush with something like "I seek the Buddha's knowledge"; rather, he got right to the punch: "I want to become a buddha."

Huilang's line, "I seek the Buddha's knowledge," gives off an unbearable smell of impurity. He doesn't say that he wants to know the Buddha; he says, "I want to know what the Buddha knows." In other words, he wants to know about the Buddha as the embodiment of understanding itself.

In response, Mazu says point-blank, "The Buddha has no knowledge," and then suggests "Don't stray from the path you're on." Buddha is not the "embodiment of understanding" that Huilang desires. Huilang flounders nervously. He's good-natured but still very immature.

If you have the time to go around acting like a gifted disciple and asking about "the Buddha's knowledge," you should spend more time sitting zazen. However, you shouldn't sit with the idea that you've got something enjoyable to look forward to. Just appreciate the act of sitting itself.

15

How Can I Become One with the Way?

A monk asked Mazu, "How can I become one with the Way?"

Mazu said, "I've never been one with the Way."

僧問、如何得合道。祖曰、我早不合道。

In asking about how to "become one with the Way," the monk is assuming that he and the Way are two different things. In saying that he's "never been one with the Way," Mazu is saying that he doesn't objectify the Way as something separate from himself.

The Way means to be yourself, here, now. The question "How can I become one with the Way?" is actually kind of grotesque; it's putting your potential way of being "out there," separate, to be stared at longingly while muttering to yourself, "I'm still astray from the true Way." The monk is trying to transcend his own existence here and now so as to apprehend a "better" way of being.

"The Way" means to be your actual, real self. If that self cannot be one with the Way, it can't be apart from the Way either.

In the poem "Dotei" ("Along the Path"), Kotaro Takamura says,

Ahead of me there is no path;
The path is made behind me.

If you already exist as yourself here and now, the issue of being one with the Way simply doesn't arise. It never enters the consciousness of a person who is already in perfect harmony with the Way. You create the path yourself as you walk forward.

I am myself, here and now. Without affirming or denying, I am creating my way of being, the Way, as I go along. If this is true, there's no need to worry about whether we're one with the Way or not; all we need to do is to enjoy the walk, including the times when we get lost and go astray.

If you get lost, you can always turn back, or ask someone for directions—or you can just stay lost if you want to. Struggles like these—wandering from the path and getting flustered, getting lost and not know-ing what to do—are all part and parcel of being alive.

16

Long and Short

A monk came and drew four lines on the ground in front of Mazu. The top line was long, and the three lines below were short.

"Don't say one line is long and three are short. Apart from words and beyond reason, Master, tell me your answer."

Mazu drew a single line on the ground and said, "Don't talk about long and short. That's my answer."

有僧於祖前作四画。上一画長、下三画短。曰、不得道一画長三画短。離四句絶百非、請和尚答某甲。祖乃画地一画曰、不得道長短。答汝了也。

Pointing to the four lines on the ground, the monk presents Mazu with a challenge: "You can't say that one line is long and three are short. So what do you say?" Mazu draws a single line and answers, "Don't talk about long and short." If there's only one line, then there is no "long" and no "short." Confronted with a distinction between long and short, Mazu responds without discrimination. Transcending the boundaries of "one" and "three," he penetrates to the very heart of things.

This is the standard interpretation, but I think it's missing something deeper.

Let's look at this dialogue in terms of the relationship between the act of *just seeing* the four lines and that of seeing them *as* "long" and "short." In seeing the four lines *as* "one long and three short," aren't we really just adding our own interpretation over and above what we actually see?

The monk, a rather brainy type, is thinking about how perception is laden with words. To him, what you are actually seeing is pure sense data; "one long and three short," on the other hand, is your own interpretation.

Mazu gives the monk's quibbling logic a swift kick in the rear. More important than the monk's riddle is the fact that to *see* is to *act*. Looking at lines on the ground means engaging them, interacting with them on a personal level—without telling stories about them being long or short. Mazu expresses this in a no-frills manner by drawing a single line.

Do not misunderstand; Mazu does not aim to draw an utterly neutral "something" that can be said to be neither long nor short. That sort of thing just doesn't exist. Instead, just draw!

It's not uncommon for Zen priests to draw a single line on the ground. The following dialogue is from *The Record of Linji*:

Linji asked the temple manager, "Where were you?"

"I was in town selling rice," he replied.

"Did you sell it all?" asked Linji.

"I sold it all."

Linji took his staff and drew a line in front of him, and asked, "And did you sell this?"

The manager let out a shout.

Linji gave him a swift thwack.

Then the head cook came along, and Linji related to him what had just transpired.

The head cook said, "The manager didn't get your meaning, Master."

"And what about you?" said Linji.

The head cook bowed reverently.

Linji gave him a thwack.

When the manager says he sold all the rice, he probably means that he literally sold all of the rice, but is that all that Linji is asking about? He is likely asking if the manager had completely sold off all of his worldly desires and attachments.

Linji draws a single line on the ground and asks, "And did you sell this?" "I get that you sold all the rice, but this is not a rice shop, and I don't think you went out for the sole purpose of selling rice," says Linji. Mere calculations and bookkeeping do not make a temple manager.

The manager shouts, and Linji delivers a blow without hesitation. Perhaps this time the thwack was an affirmation of the manager's response. "Well done. Good job."

Or maybe not. Linji of all people is not one to be so easily impressed into doling out praises. It's more likely that the manager failed the test.

Linji's line on the ground is perhaps pointing to the manager's focused mind, which is intent on selling rice. That is, he's pointing to his "rice-selling self." In this case, the manager's shout becomes a sort of protest. "By no means. I'll sell the rice, but I won't sell my mind." Linji's thwack, then, is a reprimand. "Dimwit! Your rice-selling self is just for selling rice. Once the rice is sold, you don't bring it back with you; you leave it behind. Where is your present self?"

Next, the head cook happens along, saying, "That guy just doesn't get it." Linji comes back at him with "Oh, so what about you?" The head cook bows reverently, and then *thwack*!

I don't think the second thwack is an affirmation, either. The head cook criticizes the manager based on his own misunderstanding: "A shout is hardly the appropriate response to your kind advice that even if we sell the rice, we ought not sell our mind. Is not a respectful bow more appropriate, Master?" In this case, Linji's second blow is another chastisement. "Wrong!"

Part III

Always Be Your True Self, Independent and Free

17

"Virtuous Priest—"

Zen Master Wuye of Fenzhou came to see Mazu. Observing his dignified and commanding appearance, and hearing his speech thundering out like a temple bell, Mazu said, "A towering Buddha-temple with no Buddha inside."

Wuye bowed low on his knees and asked, "I've studied nearly all of the scriptures and have a basic grasp of their meaning, but I still can't understand what is meant by the Zen saying, 'It's mind, it's Buddha.'"

Mazu said, "The very mind that can't understand is itself the Buddha; there's nothing more besides that."

Wuye asked again, "And just what is the 'mind-seal' secretly transmitted by Bodhidharma when he came from the West?"

Mazu replied, "Virtuous priest, you're trying too hard. Why don't you go, and come again some other time?"

As soon as Wuye had gotten up to leave, Mazu called him. "Virtuous priest—"

Wuye looked back at him.

"What is *this*?" said Mazu.

Wuye was suddenly enlightened, and bowed reverently.

"This dimwit! What's he bowing for?" said Mazu.

汾州無業禅師参祖。祖覩其状貌瑰偉、語音如鐘、乃曰、巍巍仏堂、其中無仏。業礼跪而問曰、三乗文學、粗窮其旨。常聞禅門即心是仏、実未能了。祖曰、只未了底心即是、更無別物。業又問、如何是祖師西来密伝心印。祖曰、大徳正鬧在。且去別時来。業纔出、祖召曰、大徳。業迴首。祖云、是什麼。業便領悟礼拝。祖云、這鈍漢、礼拝作麼。

Mazu tells Wuye that his appearance is spectacular, but his inside is less impressive. Wuye responds to Mazu's critique by admitting that he's trudged his way through the scriptures, but he still can't figure out what "It's mind, it's Buddha" is all about. Responding to Wuye's humble attitude, Mazu offers help: the very mind of yours that can't figure it out is itself the Buddha.

The enlightened mind does not exist apart from the mind that is lost and confused, nor does the mind that is lost somehow change or transform into an enlightened mind. The mind that exists here in reality as "lost" is at once none other than the buddha mind.

Mazu is kind enough to put it quite plainly, but Wuye still doesn't get it and can't help following up with a pointless question—What was it that Bodhidharma transmitted?—at which point Mazu chases him off. Dejected, Wuye turns to leave. Mazu calls after him. Without thinking, Wuye turns back toward him. Perceiving the opportunity present, Mazu speaks into it: "What is *this*?" What is it that just turned to look at Mazu? The mind lost in delusion? The mind of the Buddha?

Mazu sees when Wuye has been enlightened. "It sure took you long enough! And now you bow!" Not the best approval one can receive, but an approval nonetheless.

In the Zen world, you don't take your time in responding when someone calls to you. If someone calls out "Yahooo!" you respond with no-self, like a mountain echo: "Yahooo!" Even so, turning around when someone calls after you is one of the basics of human relationships. Wuye's reaction when Mazu calls him "virtuous priest" could be a mere conditioned response.

18

"Lecture Master—"

Lecture Master Liang came to see Mazu. Mazu asked him, "I hear that your lectures on the scriptures and commentaries are quite good. Is this true?"

"Oh, I wouldn't go that far," said Liang.

"And what do you use to lecture?"

"I use my mind to lecture."

Mazu said, "The mind is like an actor, and thought like a clown. How can you explain the scriptures?"

Liang replied angrily, "If the mind can't lecture, then I suppose you'd suggest that nothingness can?"

"In fact, nothing is quite good at lecturing," said Mazu.

Unable to assent, Liang went out and started down the stairs.

Mazu called after him. "Lecture master—"

Without a thought, Liang turned to face him, and was suddenly enlightened. He immediately bowed reverently.

"This crazy monk! What's he bowing for?" said Mazu.

Liang returned to his temple and addressed the monks there. "I thought that no one could better me when it came to lecturing on scriptures and their interpretations, but today, one word from Master Mazu has smashed to pieces all that I've done up until now."

Liang immediately retired to the Western Mountains and was never heard from again.

亮座主参祖。祖問曰、見説座主大講得経論、是否。
亮云、不敢。祖曰、将甚麼講。亮云、将心講。祖曰、心
如工伎児、意如和伎者。争解得経。亮抗声云、心既講
不得、虛空莫講得麼。祖曰、却是虛空講得。亮不肯、
便出、将下階。祖召云、座主。亮回首、豁然大悟、便
礼拝。祖曰、這鈍根阿師、礼拝作麼。亮帰寺、告聴衆
曰、某甲所講経論、謂無人及得、今日被馬大師一問、
平生工夫氷消瓦解。径入西山更無蹤跡。

Lecture masters' tendency to intellectualize generally lands them the role of getting beaten by Zen teachers.

When Mazu greets Lecture Master Liang by complimenting him on his lectures, Liang appears to be humble—though perhaps he is just making a show of his humility. On the inside, he holds his fair share of pride. Aiming to turn down Liang's stuck-up nose, Mazu asks, "And what do you use to teach?" Liang replies, "I use my mind."

When he puts on the air of a dignified teacher and begins to lecture, the "mind" he uses is the actor-mind, the mind occupied with maintaining a certain role. Actors do no more than put on a performance. While playing teacher, his performing mind exists separate from his true mind. And as for the actual content of his lectures, they're no more than a preconceived script.

Liang was likely a charismatic teacher. It seems that Mazu, having heard of his reputation, cautions him that his splendid lectures are no more than a play. Even if he claims to speak from his heart, that "mind" is nothing but a hack actor, calculating the effect of his performance.

Liang, the performer in question, is infatuated with the false image of himself as a passionate, hard-working teacher. Mazu hits this hidden self-deception square in the face, suggesting that nothingness would be a better teaching than Liang's farcical role-playing.

Mazu calls out after the indignant Liang as he turns to leave, "Lecture master—." Lecture Master Liang has been playing teacher and looking down on everyone with a come-and-behold-my-famous-performance attitude, but when Mazu suddenly calls after him, in that unexpected moment he forgets his act altogether. Absentmindedly, naively, he turns around, forgetting himself to the point that he even pays obeisance and bows.

When someone unexpectedly calls out your name, there is something in you that automatically responds. Through his unconditioned response, Liang suddenly becomes aware of his unadorned self, not the actor. The one responsible for this feat of discovery is none other than Liang himself. It isn't Mazu at all.

Everyone, in their "suchness," is a buddha. When you realize that your own mind is a buddha, the Buddha's own self-awareness is in effect. No one taught this to you. When Liang bows to Mazu as if he had been taught something, he extinguishes the nice self-awareness that just occurred. There's no need to bow, but he does it anyway, because the effect of his realization has not completely taken hold.

Mazu's final statement feels like a teasing, bitter laugh. Liang ends up defeated, with a complete loss of self-confidence. Mazu's way can be rather harsh.

When called upon, you turn around without a thought. This mind is the "Buddha" of "It's mind, it's Buddha." When called upon suddenly, you don't think, "Ah. I have to turn around now." This mind is none other than Buddha.

19

Call and Response

A scholar-priest came to visit and asked, "Exactly what sort of teachings are transmitted in Zen, anyway?"

Mazu responded by asking, "What sort of teachings do you transmit, Lecture Master?"

"I lecture on a little over twenty sutras and commentaries."

"So, you're a lion!"

"Oh, I wouldn't go that far," said the lecture master.

Mazu gave a deep, guttural shout.

"That's a teaching," said the lecture master.

"What sort of teaching?" asked Mazu.

"The lion coming out of the cave."

Mazu was silent.

"This is also a teaching."

"What sort of teaching?" asked Mazu.

"The lion in the cave."

"And that which neither goes out nor comes in—what sort of teaching would that be?" asked Mazu.

The lecture master had no reply.

The lecture master said farewell and was about to go out through the doors when Mazu called after him: "Lecture Master—"

The lecture master turned around.

"What's *this*?"

The lecture master had no reply.

"This crazy monk!" said Mazu.

有講僧来問曰、未審禅宗伝持何法。祖却問曰、座主伝持何法。主曰、忝講得経論二十余本。祖曰、莫是獅子児否。主曰、不敢。祖作嘘嘘声。主曰、此是法。祖曰、是甚麼法。主曰、獅子出窟法。祖乃默然。主曰、此亦是法。祖曰、是甚麼法。主曰、獅子在窟法。祖曰、不出不入、是甚麼法。主無対。遂辞出門、祖召曰、座主。主回首。祖曰、是甚麼。主亦無対。祖曰、這鈍根阿師。

Mazu asks the question, "What sort of teaching?" three times. The first two times, the lecture master manages to follow Mazu's line of questioning, but neither of his answers gets to the heart of the matter. By the third time, he's at a loss for words.

Mazu is kind enough to give him another chance. As the lecture master is about to leave, Mazu calls after him, and then asks, "What's this?" when the lecture master turns around. That is, "Why did you turn around? What kind of teaching did you think it was when you turned around just now? I'm not trying to 'teach' you anything at all."

Even though the lecture master is a rather hardheaded academic, Mazu still gives him all the kindness he can. The lecture master needs to achieve realization for himself. When Mazu calls after him, it's no more than an opportunity for the lecture master's self-awareness to awaken.

He is not trying to give a reasoned argument along the lines of "The one who turns around when called after is none other than the Buddha." Rather, Mazu wants the person being called after to realize that the here-and-now phenomenon of turning around when called is itself Buddha. This call-and-turn phenomenon happens when someone else calls upon you and you respond completely naturally, without conscious effort, to the action.

Even the overly intellectual lecture master has a self who responds when called upon. When we respond to the call by turning around, there is no cause-and-effect thought process wherein we decide, "I've been called upon. Thus, I must turn about." The important thing is that we just turn around.

Mazu does not explain a single thing in this dialogue. The exchange that occurs between Mazu and the lecture master is not something to be made subject to interpretation.

Even so, the lecture master, perhaps because it's just his nature, interprets everything that Mazu says and does as "a teaching." He's all caught up in the idea that if he interprets something it means that he's understood it, that every scenario is something to be interpreted and comprehended. Finally, even Mazu's supply of patience runs out, and he lets him go, saying, "What a fool."

Mazu uses the same device three times in a row, calling his visitors from behind as they turn to leave. All three of them happen to be intellectuals: Wuye the monk is puffed up and impressive looking; Lecture Master Liang is a veteran teacher with a widespread reputation for lecturing on the scriptures and commentaries; and the present lecture master is also an academic, with his "I lecture on a little over twenty sutras and commentaries."

After some degree of study, the misconception that "I understand Zen" arises in the student. Such a student can talk about fine wine, but he or she has never actually tasted it. Encountering these types, Mazu brings out his secret weapon, calling on them at their moment of departure.

In the instant where you turn around when called upon, your true flesh-and-blood self is laid bare; all the open books on your desk do you no good in this moment. Into that unguarded moment, Mazu thrusts the question, "Who are you?" At this point, the person called upon has a surprising tendency to awaken to their raw self, empty of content, and become flustered. When, still flustered, they bow in deference, Mazu hits them again: "What are you bowing for?" he says. "Are you sure that's what you want to do?"

Practicing Zen means being your true self at all times. Simple conditioned responses won't do; if you bow, that's fine, but you'd better be sure that you're doing it with your whole being. If not, Mazu isn't going to let you off the hook so easily.

20

Can You Drink the River Dry?

Layman Pang asked Mazu, "What sort of a person is the one who has no involvement with the ten thousand dharmas?"

Mazu said, "Drink up all the water in the West River in a single gulp, and I'll tell you."

龐居士問祖云、不与万法為侶者、是甚麼人。祖曰、待汝一口吸尽西江水、即向汝道。

The "ten thousand dharmas" means all existence; the "one who has no involvement" with all existence refers to an ungraspable absolute. Just to ask about such a thing is like rejecting an answer before one is even given.

Mazu responds to Pang's impossible question by giving him the ridiculous task of drinking all the water in the West River in a single gulp. Is this impossible assignment just an excuse for Mazu not to answer? I don't think so. Mazu is telling Layman Pang that one thing can't swallow up all of existence.

Things and people exist in relation to one another; they are never "absolute." There's always going to be something that you can't consume unto yourself. For example, says Mazu, "Can you drink the West River dry?" Just as that's impossible, it's also impossible to exist without being involved with anything that is other than oneself. Swallowing up all that is other so that all that exists within *you*, so that you become the absolute, is something that just can't be done. "If you think you can, though, go ahead and show me," says Mazu.

What about Layman Pang's question? Is it just a stupid question that he shouldn't have asked in the first place? I wouldn't go that far. Pang's question has a certain charm, which lies in the human aspect that might be termed a "place of nothingness," a place that *does* seem to encompass everything.

However, taking in this somewhat fascinating question, Mazu's reply says: I don't think that this "place of nothingness" is a *person*.

The philosopher Blaise Pascal said that humans are "thinking reeds." Physically speaking, we are weak, like reeds swaying in the wind. These reeds, however, can think. In thought, in consciousness, we swallow up all of creation.

Immanuel Kant said that all objects are objects of consciousness. Subjectivity swallows up all of objective existence through concepts, yet subjectivity does not itself exist objectively. Objectivity and subjectivity do not have an objective relationship with one another.

If this is all true, then just what is this thing we call "consciousness?" Is it a "person" who exists?

A "person" who has absolutely no involvement with all of existence cannot exist in this world. In addition to existing in the world, you also must be involved with "other" things and people existing here. When Mazu suggests, "When the impossible happens, I'll tell you," he's being quite sincere. Mazu asks Pang to suppose that there really is something or someone who transcends all of existence. Would that really be his ideal?

One that has no involvement with all that exists is one that has completely swallowed everything up, one that retreats entirely into subjective reality. Asking about this existence in which there are no "others" in terms of personhood is to put your own existence in danger. Despite that, Layman Pang carelessly lets out with this rather extreme question that pops into his mind.

Pang is a man of good potential. In pursuing this sort of question, he puts himself at the crossroads of life and death but doesn't realize it. Will he go right, or left?

21

Forget Bodhidharma, What about You?

Someone asked, "What is the meaning of Bodhidharma's coming from the West?"

Mazu responded, "What does this mean, here and now?"

問、如何是西来意。祖曰、即今是甚麼意。

Mazu, presented with a question about the "meaning" of Bodhidharma's coming to China from the West (India), questions the questioner: "Forget Bodhidharma, what does it mean that *you* are here, *now*?" Don't worry about other people. What about you, yourself?

In answering a question with another question, perhaps Mazu is saying, "You have to answer that for yourself. No one else can do it for you."

The question posed to Mazu is about what it means to be a Zen practitioner in the present, here and now. Perhaps latent in the question is the idea that to practice Zen is to embody the life of Bodhidharma, as to be a Christian is on some level to embody the life of Christ.

The event of Bodhidharma's coming from the West is not just a simple historical fact. No matter how much you boil the event down, his coming never crystallizes into a "meaning" that embodies the very essence of Zen. The event of Bodhidharma's coming only has meaning insofar as it serves as an opportunity to awaken a consciousness of eternity in this self, who exists only and always in the here and now.

Bodhidharma came over from India—an event from the distant past. But the meaning of it is not that of an event in the distant past; it's the meaning of your present state of being, of that which is constituted by the here and now.

The difficulty of comprehending the "meaning" of Bodhidharma's coming from the West was the same for Zen practitioners living in Mazu's time as it was for those living while Bodhidharma was still alive. The living, breathing *you* stands before Bodhidharma. To grasp the meaning of Bodhidharma's coming from the West is to grasp the here and now of the *you* who grasps.

22

Your Own Treasure

It was Dazhu Huihai's first time receiving teaching from Mazu.

Mazu asked, "Where did you come from?"

"From Great Cloud Temple in Yuezhou."

"And what are you looking to do here?"

"I come seeking the Buddhadharma."

Mazu said, "You have a great store of treasure in your own house, yet you are throwing it away, running about here and there. What are you doing? I don't have anything here. What sort of Buddhadharma are you seeking?"

Dazhu bowed, and then asked, "What is this 'treasure in my own house'?"

"The one asking me at this moment, you, are that treasure. You have all the tools you need and lack nothing; you can use it all freely. There's no need to seek anything outside."

Hearing this, Dazhu suddenly awakened to his true mind and danced for joy, giving thanks.

大珠初参祖。祖問曰、従何処来。曰、越州大雲寺来。
祖曰、来此擬須何事。曰、来求仏法。祖曰、自家宝蔵
不顧、抛家散走作什麼。我這裏一物也無。求甚麼仏
法。珠遂礼拝　問曰、阿那箇是慧海自家宝蔵。祖曰、
即今問我者、是汝宝蔵。一切具足、更無欠少、使用自
在。何假向外求覓。珠於言下、自識本心。不由知覚、
踊躍礼謝。

If you stop to consider that you actually exist as *you*,
as opposed to one of the other myriad possibilities of
what you could have been, your existence is more or
less a miracle. If your parents hadn't met, you wouldn't
have been born, and if their parents hadn't met, they
wouldn't have been born either, and so on, ad infinitum. For your particular blend of genes to come into
existence, the event of your birth was brought about
by a long string of coincidences piled up one on top
of the other; the further back you look, the more and
more scant the probability becomes. It really is tempt-
ing to call it a miracle, but if we do, then the world is
just a big mess of miracles.

Indeed, in the entire world there's not another person like you. In that sense, you are "special," but you
don't need anything more than common sense to figure that out. And the fact that you are you is the same
as the fact that anyone is anyone. If you go around calling yourself a miracle, you're just making yourself out
to be more important than everyone else.

Mazu says that although it's no particular miracle
that you are you, it *is* a special treasure as far as you

yourself are concerned. Take on this self of yours just as it is. There's no need to go looking for anything outside.

There is a Zen saying from Master Yunmen, *Nichi nichi kore ko niche*, or "Every day is a good day." For Zen practitioners who live out this sentiment, everything is special—a rock, a flower petal, even the person who is looking at them. When everything is special in this way, there is actually nothing at all that's special.

It is nonetheless possible to live out the attitude that "Every day is a good day." Regardless of what happens, all you need to do to face any situation positively is to decide to do so. This is a freedom shared by everyone.

If you decide that you are a special case among unremarkable cases, though, it will become very difficult to live out an attitude of kindness.

Everything is special, but because of this, nothing is in fact special. There is nothing that is not special or one of a kind. All we really need to do is accept everyone and everything just as they are.

23

A Swift Kick

Master Shuilao of Hongzhou, on his first visit to Mazu, asked, "What is the most essential meaning of Bodhidharma's coming from the West?"

"Show reverence," said Mazu.

As soon as Shuilao bowed, Mazu kicked him over.

Shuilao was thoroughly enlightened. He stood up, clapped his hands, and bellowed out laughing, "How wonderful! How wonderful! A hundred thousand samadhis and the most mysterious teachings—I've seen their root in the tip of a single strand of hair!"

He made obeisance and took his leave.

Some time later, he declared to his monks, "Ever since I took that kick from Master Ma, and even now, I haven't stopped laughing."

洪州水老和尚、初参祖問、如何是西來的的意。祖云、礼拜著。老纔礼拝、祖便与一蹋。老大悟。起来撫掌、呵呵大笑云、也大奇、也大奇、百千三昧、無量妙義、

只向一毛頭上便識得根源去。便礼拝而退。後告衆
云、自従一喫馬師蹹、直至如今笑不休。

Shuilao asks about Bodhidharma's intention in coming to China. Mazu orders him to show reverence and
then gives him a horse-kick as soon as he bows.

The question of the "meaning of Bodhidharma's
coming from the West" is not about the intent behind
someone else's actions; it has nothing to do with
Bodhidharma. It's about fully believing that your mind
is none other than that of a buddha. The answer is not
to be understood with the head; it is something that
must be absorbed through experience, through trial
and difficulty.

Mazu tells Shuilao to show reverence, and he
directly complies. Admirably obedient. So why, if
he does just as he's told, does he find himself on the
receiving end of Mazu's kick?

Bowing to the master is, in this case, proper eti-
quette. However, Shuilao's way of answer-seeking here
also betrays a rather shameless attitude, i.e., shirking
responsibility for your own dilemma and leaving it to
the master to solve.

Shuilao gets a kick not in spite of his obedience, but
rather *because* of it. Mazu's kick is saying, "Problems
dealing with the root of things can only be solved by
yourself. Don't show up expecting an answer from me."

Shuilao asks a very earnest question about Bodhidharma's coming from the West. Perhaps, when Mazu
suddenly tells him to bow, Shuilao feels slighted. Even
so, Shuilao at his core wants to do what's right and so

complies. As he bows, perhaps the expression on his face betrays his feeling, and—Pow! He gets punted.

As he is kicked over Shuilao suddenly discovers his current state of being: his slighted self. It may have been a self that was feeling annoyed and dejected, but in any case, he discovers his self.

The most essential lessons in life cannot be learned from someone else—you have to figure them out for yourself. When Shuilao gets kicked, he suddenly realizes, "Oh, so *this* is who I am! Ha!" When he later says that he still hasn't stopped laughing, maybe he means that ever since that time he's just been being himself.

24

Withdraw Your Legs

One day, Yinfeng was pushing the waste cart, and Mazu was sitting with his legs extended out in the road.

"Pardon me, Master—please withdraw your legs," said Yinfeng.

"What's already extended cannot be withdrawn," said Mazu.

"What's already proceeding cannot be turned back," said Yinfeng. So he proceeded with the cart, running over Mazu's legs and injuring them badly.

Mazu went back to the Dharma hall, took up an axe, and said, "Let the one who just ran over this old priest's legs come forward."

Yinfeng came right up and stretched out his neck before Mazu.

Mazu put down the axe.

峰一日推土車次、祖展脚在路上坐。峰云、請師收足。祖云、已展不收。峰云、已進不退。乃推車、碾過祖脚損。帰法堂、執斧子云、適来碾損老僧脚底出来。峰便出、於祖前引頸。祖乃置斧。

Two children are bickering. They get in a fight over some trivial matter, and before they know it they can't stop. The argument continues to heat up until one of them sticks out their face saying, "Fine, why don't you hit me?" But the smack never comes. "Whatever," says the other as he turns around and leaves.

Yinfang is a pretty straight-laced individual; he lacks flexibility. Mazu decides to have some fun with him. "Let's see just how stubborn you really are." He finds out.

Ordered to come forward in the Dharma hall, Yinfang presents his neck to Mazu. Does he mean it as an apology? Or is it more of a taunt? Or is it something else? "If you think you can cut off my head, let's see you do it."

Mazu can't follow through with his threat; he's holding an axe. Maybe he should have picked up a staff instead. He grabbed the wrong tool; he brought something he can't actually use, but the situation demands that he follow through. Seeing that Mazu has an axe, Yinfang presents his neck. "Let's see if you can chop it off." It's like they're playing chicken.

However you spin it, running over someone's legs with a waste cart is just cruel. Starting something and then seeing it through to the end is a good thing, but it's not necessary to injure someone in order to do so. If it's not necessary, it's to be avoided. When Mazu puts down the axe, he makes an elegant demonstration of how to turn back before things go too far.

25

What If I Pretend to Be Enlightened?

A junior monk named Danyuan returned from a pilgrimage. He drew a circle before Mazu, made obeisance next to it, and stood up again.

Mazu said, "So you want to become a buddha, then?"

"I don't even know how to rub my eyes."

Mazu said, "I don't measure up to you."

The young priest was lost for words.

有小師耽源、行脚回、於祖前画箇円相、就上拝了立。祖曰、汝莫欲作仏否。曰、某甲不解捏目。祖曰、吾不如汝。小師不対。

Wittgenstein says that a dog can't believably pretend to be hurt. Teaching a dog to put on such a good show that no one could ever tell that the pain wasn't real would be a difficult task.

The inexperienced junior monk Danyuan draws a circle before Mazu, bows, and stands up—a very meaningful series of actions, or so it would seem. For a Zen monk, a circle is a symbol of the perfectly harmonious world, of all of existence. The additional act of faking obeisance was a bluff, a challenge for Mazu. He's pretending to be enlightened.

"You're already a buddha, yet you want to become one?" asks Mazu. Changing in order to become what you already are wouldn't be easy.

"I don't even know how to rub my eyes," says Danyuan. You rub your eyes when you want to be able to see more clearly. Danyuan is denying Mazu's suggestion that he wants to become a buddha: "I hold no such lofty aspirations." He's pretending to be modest.

If we take Mazu's reply, "I don't measure up to you," at face value, it seems that he's affirming the junior monk's answer. "Nice work!"

But Danyuan doesn't know how to respond to Mazu's affirmation. It becomes clear that his exemplary answer, "I don't even know how to rub my eyes," was memorized straight from the textbook. Danyuan pretends to be enlightened, but he gets himself in trouble at the critical moment. If you want to succeed at faking something, you need to make sure you have enough skill not to be found out.

Maybe he heard some sarcasm in Mazu's flattering "I don't measure up to you." The exaggerated compliment burst his bubble, making him feel ashamed, like he was still just a kid. "Maybe he knows!" Danyuan's performance comes to an end.

26

A Letter with a Circle

Mazu sent a monk to deliver a letter to Master Qin of Jingshan. In the letter, he drew a single circle. Master Qin opened the letter, took a brush, and put a dot in the center. Later on, one of the monks related these events to Nanyang Huizhong. Huizhong said, "That Jingshan, he fell for Mazu's set-up."

祖令僧馳書与径山欽和尚。書中画一円相。径山纔開見、索筆於中著一点。後有僧挙似忠国師。国師云、欽師猶被馬師惑。

As a symbol of the entire universe, the circle is infinite. Since the universe has no definite borders, it also has no definite center. In a sense, any given point could be the center.

In a finite circle, there is only one center. It's possible to draw a dot there if you like. In an infinite circle, there are an infinite number of centers, so you can't very well represent them, within the symbol of a *finite* circle, with a dot. If Mazu's circle was a symbol of the world, it is completely full of centers. You don't draw a dot in that sort of symbolic circle.

Mazu draws his circle without a dot. It's a symbol of the infinitely vast universe. "Don't go around drawing circles without a center," says Jingshan when he draws the dot. "You can't draw an infinitely vast circle, so please stop drawing things that can't be drawn."

Mazu decides to symbolize this unrepresentable, infinite circle by drawing a finite circle. Just to make it clear that it represents an infinite circle, he deliberately omits the dot from the center—a traditional way of symbolizing the infinite.

It's also possible that Jingshan took the circle that Mazu drew as a symbol of consciousness rather than of the universe. Consciousness can travel anywhere it pleases, so it's acceptable to represent it as a circle having infinite size. However, consciousness is something that belongs to a particular person, i.e., to "me." That "me" is at the center of the circle—so Jingshan puts a dot in the circle to make a place for that "me."

In the real world, though, the center does not exist only as "me." There are innumerable "me's" everywhere. Everywhere, there is a center. If that's the case, then just putting a single dot in the center is not going to work.

When Jingshan makes the dot that he ought not make, it shows that Mazu has taken him in. If you get a letter from someone like Mazu, even if it just contains a simple circle, you can't help thinking that it represents something deep and meaningful. But if you do see it as automatically profound, it only goes to show that you've already been led astray.

Perhaps Mazu and Jingshan share a mutual understanding and are just having fun together. Perhaps Jingshan intentionally made it look like he got taken in. If so, then the one who got taken in wasn't Jingshan at all. It was Huizhong.

Part IV

Your Mind Is Buddha

27

I'll Do It My Way, Thanks

Zen Master Fachang of Great Plum Mountain came to see Mazu for the first time and asked, "What is the Buddha like?"

Mazu said, "It's mind, it's Buddha."

Fachang was suddenly enlightened.

Later on, Fachang went to Great Plum Mountain. Mazu heard that Master Fachang had a temple there, so Mazu sent a monk to ask him, "Master, what did you acquire from Mazu that you now have a temple on this mountain?"

Fachang said, "Mazu told me, 'It's mind, it's Buddha.' Now I have a temple on this mountain."

The monk said, "Mazu has recently been teaching a different Buddhadharma."

"How is it different?" said Fachang.

The monk said, "Recently he's been saying 'Not mind, not Buddha.'"

"That old geezer! There's no end to his trying to confuse people. Even if he is saying 'Not mind, not Buddha,' I'm sticking with 'It's mind, it's Buddha.'"

The monk returned to Mazu and told him what happened.

"The plum is ripe," said Mazu.

大梅山法常禅師、初参祖問、如何是仏。祖云、即心是仏。常即大悟。後居大梅山。祖聞師住山、乃令一僧到問云、和尚見馬師、得箇什麼便住此山。常云、馬師向我道即心是仏。我便向這裏住。僧云、馬師近日仏法又別。常云、作麼生別。僧云、近日又道非心非仏。常云、這老漢惑乱人、未有了日。任汝非心非仏、我只管即心即仏。其僧回挙似祖。祖云、梅子熟也。

"It's mind, it's Buddha" means that your ordinary mind, just so, is none other than the Buddha. This is none other than the mind stained by worldly passions, by joy, anger, sorrow, and pleasure. Worldly passions and *bodhi* are equal, the same.

It seems, though, that Mazu had just changed his core teaching from "It's mind, it's Buddha" to "Not mind, not Buddha."

Enlightenment transcends reason, just as your instinct to cuddle a cute baby involves no reason. Beyond reason, beyond your rational mind, "It's mind, it's Buddha" is no different from "Not mind, not Buddha."

When Mazu told Fachang, "It's mind, it's Buddha," he became enlightened. Although Mazu provides the opportunity for enlightenment, it's not as if he *bestows* it upon Fachang. Fachang acquires "It's mind, it's Buddha" for himself.

When Mazu changes his teaching from "It's mind, it's Buddha" to "Not mind, not Buddha," it's Mazu's problem. It has nothing to do with Fachang. For Fachang, "It's mind, it's Buddha" is an unshakable fact of his very being.

"It's mind, it's Buddha" stands on the simple premise that "You are the master of your own life." To do, or not to do: there is a decision to be made. That decision always belongs to no one but you. Even if it turns out to be the worst decision in the world, the one who made it was you, yourself. You can't blame it on anyone else.

When you find yourself facing an urgent problem, all you can do is work it out in your own way. When Fachang hears that Mazu has changed his core teaching to "Not mind, not Buddha," he has all the more reason to follow through with "It's mind, it's Buddha."

"Not mind, not Buddha" is not just a simple negation of "It's mind, it's Buddha." "It's mind, it's Buddha" means that "Mind is Buddha." A proper negation would be something more like "Mind is not Buddha." Instead, "Not mind, not Buddha" means that it's not mind, nor is it Buddha. But what is "it"? What is it that is not mind and not Buddha? Fachang, with his "Even if Mazu is saying 'Not mind, not Buddha,' I'm still staying with 'It's mind, it's Buddha'" tells us it's the not-twoness of the whole. But if that is indeed Fachang's reason for sticking with "It's mind, it's Buddha," then why has Mazu switched to "Not mind, not Buddha?"

To say "It's mind, it's Buddha" and "Not mind, not Buddha" are just two sides of the same coin is a false reading of the change in Mazu's terminology. It's not about how a thing's appearance changes depending on your viewpoint. "Not mind, not Buddha" is expressing the possibility that when something exists as "not mind," it also exists at the same time as "not Buddha."

In Chinese, the phrases "It's mind, it's Buddha" and "Not mind, not Buddha" have no subject. Since Fachang asks, "What is the Buddha?" we are naturally inclined to think that Mazu's answer is saying, "The Buddha is . . . ," but that's just his point. Mazu is simply saying, "It's mind, it's Buddha" and "Not mind, not Buddha." Buddha is not something that can be defined or taken up as an object for discussion.

If you get too hung up on the fact that mind is Buddha, you're liable to forget that mind is not Buddha. Even if mind and Buddha are identical, their identity itself (the actual thing that is called both mind and buddha) is neither mind nor Buddha. "But if you put all that into words, you ruin it," says Fachang. "You've understood well," Mazu seems to reply.

"It's mind, it's Buddha" and "Not mind, not Buddha" are really just empty phrases—even more meaningless are the smaller phrases "it's mind" and "not mind."

Any talk concerning the Buddha is bound to come up short. If you can't say it well, it's better to just keep silent.

28

To Stop Children's Crying

A monk asked Mazu, "Master, why do you teach, 'It's mind, it's Buddha'?"

Mazu said, "To make children stop crying."

"And what about when they stop crying?"

Mazu said, "Not mind, not Buddha."

"And how do you direct people who are neither of these two types?"

Mazu said, "I tell them that it's not a thing."

"And if you happen to meet someone who is enlightened?"

Mazu said, "I just have them embody the Great Way."

僧問、和尚為甚麼説即心即仏。祖曰、為止小児啼。曰、啼止時如何。祖曰、非心非仏。曰、除此二種、人来如何指示。祖曰、向伊道不是物。曰、忽遇其中人来時如何。祖曰、且教伊体会大道。

Monks, like children, tend to seek the Buddha as an object, and if you don't pay children any attention, they won't stop pestering you. To quiet them down, you say, "It's mind, it's Buddha." Your mind is Buddha just as it is, even if you aren't seeking Buddha.

When a child can't quit his or her anxious seeking, you calm and comfort the child, saying, "Mind is Buddha." This is just a temporary measure, the most expedient means for the moment—like giving a crying baby a rattle.

After "It's mind, it's Buddha" has satisfied the child and calmed them down a bit, you tell say, "Actually, it's not mind, nor is it Buddha." In "It's mind, it's Buddha," that "mind" is not mind, nor is that "Buddha," Buddha. "It" is not something that can be objectified and spoken about. That's why Mazu plainly concludes, "It's not a thing."

The reason that we can say, "It's mind, it's Buddha" (in spite of the fact that mind is mind and Buddha is Buddha) is this: it's also "Not mind, not Buddha." Since "mind" is not mind, and "Buddha" is not Buddha, we can say, "It's mind, it's Buddha." It makes sense that "mind" is "Buddha" only because "not mind" is "not Buddha."

The morning star = the evening star. They appear to be two different things, but in truth the two are both the planet Venus. However, without making some qualifications, we cannot make the statement that the morning star, the evening star, and Venus are all the same thing. The morning star and the evening star are both Venus, but the evening star is not at once the morning star. This is what allows us to say, "The morning star = the evening star." The morning star and the evening star exist in a not-two relationship, a relationship in which two related things are neither completely identical nor completely separate.

If we were to force a question about the "it's" of "It's mind, it's Buddha," we would be asking about the mind and the Buddha's identity. Identity, though, is not a concrete object and so can't be sought or grasped through objective forms of seeking and questioning. All we can say about it is that it's "Not mind, not Buddha." If you want to take it to the extreme and say that these two statements are the same, then you end up having to say "It's 'It's mind, it's Buddha', it's 'Not mind, not Buddha'" as well as "Not 'It's mind, it's Buddha,' not 'Not mind, not Buddha,'" and so on, ad infinitum.

Perhaps Fachang in the previous episode was wise for planting his feet firmly on the ground of "It's mind, it's Buddha."

The issue is with the "it." When we say, "It's mind, it's Buddha," we have a mind and Buddha that have been objectified for the sake of conversation. I suppose this points to their two-ness. To point to their one-ness, we need "not mind, not Buddha." In saying this, we remove mind and Buddha as objects of conversation, and we are left with mind and Buddha in their not-twoness.

Setting up the words "mind" and "Buddha" and saying that "It's mind, it's Buddha" and "Not mind, not Buddha" leads to all sorts of confusion. Mind and Buddha are not-two. Mind and Buddha are not objective "things"; that's why Mazu plainly concludes, "It's not a thing."

Let's get to know this expression, "It's not a thing," by taking a look at koan 27 from *The Gateless Gate*:

A monk asked Master Nanquan, "Is there a teaching that you haven't explained to anyone?"

"Yes," said Nanquan.

"And what is this teaching that you haven't explained to anyone?"

Nanquan said, "Not mind, not Buddha, not a thing."

When the monk asks Nanquan if he has any teachings that he hasn't explained to anyone, he probably wants to hear "No." Instead, he gets an unexpected "Yes." What the monk doesn't realize is that Nanquan's answer here *is* the teaching that he hasn't explained to anyone.

The unexplainable teaching exists in a realm that transcends the elements that compose our world. As soon as that teaching is explained as "Not mind, not Buddha, not a thing," it ceases being the teaching. Nanquan, in response to this unanswerable question about the unexplainable teaching, goes ahead and answers, "Yes." On top of that, he superfluously adds that it's not mind, not Buddha, and not a thing. "It's not anything that can possibly be conceived of."

The unexplainable teaching's merit is that it cannot be explained. When you are able to taste it just-so in its inexpressibility then, like a dream becoming reality, it becomes possible to describe things beyond the objective world.

When you negate all of existence completely, you find yourself fluttering toward affirmation. Indeed, absolute negation equals absolute affirmation. But negation doesn't stop at just "Not mind, not Buddha, not a thing." No matter how many things you rattle off saying, "It's not this, not this," you never reach an answer as to what *it* actually is.

Being and nonbeing become issues because things that "are" and "are not" *can* be spoken of and thought about. That which goes beyond being and nonbeing can be neither spoken of nor thought about. When it comes to these things, all you can do is remain silent. Even if you make a long list of things that can be neither spoken of nor conceived, and then say "It's not quite any of these things," you still haven't managed to speak or think about it directly.

Saying that the unexplainable teaching *exists* amounts to the same thing as saying that it doesn't. When the monk hears Nanquan's "Yes," he takes it as a relative yes (as *opposed* to no) answer. He then follows up with "If yes, then what is it?" Nanquan would be perfectly justified in ignoring him at this point, but his kindness leads him to say, "It's not this, not that, and not anything."

29

Why Does a Boat Float in Water?

Layman Pang asked Mazu, "Though water has no muscles or bones, it can support an enormous boat. What sort of reasoning does this follow?"

Mazu said, "There's no water here, and no boat either. What are you talking about with these 'muscles and bones'?"

問、如水無筋骨、能勝万斛舟、此理如何。祖曰、這裏無水亦無舟。説甚麼筋骨。

Both boats and water exist in their own peculiar way. You may know that there is some law of mechanics that explains it all, but you probably don't actually know how an enormous boat can float on water. If you want to know, you can study physics. If you're not willing to study but want to know the answers anyway, you might just be lazy.

Things exist as a "self" simultaneous to other things that exist as "others." Water has its existence as water, and boats exist as boats, and they relate to each other accordingly. Layman Pang wants to somehow clarify the workings of this self/other relationship.

Pang submits the example of a boat bobbing up and down on the waves, but Mazu won't have it. "Is that something you really need to be asking?" he says. "If it's really such a vital question and you are seeking a deep and profound answer, are you sure you want to attempt conceiving of this relationship between boat and water, making it into a half-baked abstraction?"

I wonder if Pang didn't have a proud "right answer" ready at hand. Perhaps he had planned on popping his question, then moving in with his prepared response if Mazu wasn't able to answer it. Certainly testing others to see if they know something that you know is not great behavior. Still, Mazu, whether he's aware of Pang's hidden intentions or not, passes with flying colors. "How would I know about the rationale of water and boat?"

30

I Want To, But Is It Okay?

Lianshi of Hongzhou asked, "Should I partake of wine and meat, or is it better to abstain?"

Mazu said, "To partake is your present happiness, to abstain is your future blessing."

洪州廉使問曰、喫酒肉即是、不喫即是。祖曰、若喫是中丞禄、不喫是中丞福。

Lianshi is a public official, traveling from place to place checking for political corruption. His line of work requires a person with integrity.

The earnest and trustworthy Lianshi is troubled over the issue of whether or not it is acceptable for him to drink wine and eat meat. He wants to have a drink now and then. He wants to eat meat from time to time. Still, he wants to do what's right, and he knows that

Buddhism forbids meat and alcohol, so he finds himself hesitant to indulge.

One interpretation of Mazu's response may be that since Lianshi's not a monk, he can technically do as he pleases, but it's better to avoid wine and meat. All Mazu says, however, is that if you partake of meat and wine, you'll enjoy the taste in this life, and if you abstain, you'll enjoy blessing in the next. He makes no comment as to whether or not it's acceptable for him to partake. Eating and drinking will give you happiness, and abstaining will give you happiness, too. "Do as you like," says Mazu.

Straight-laced people like Lianshi tend to set the hurdles extra high for themselves and then become troubled that they aren't able—or won't be able—to clear them. You may laugh, but the person in question feels sincerely troubled. When the hurdle is too high to jump over, one insightful solution is just to duck right under it. This is sometimes called "taking a courageous retreat," but for people like Lianshi, that's not an easy thing to do.

For the happy, the world is a happy place. For the unhappy, it's an unhappy place. You are not simply a single element of the world; you yourself constitute a premise concerning "the way things are."

Happiness and unhappiness are not characteristics of the world "out there." They are predicated on you, the subject. "Go ahead and be happy!" says Mazu.

31

Someone's Listening!

Zen Master Fahui of Letan asked Mazu, "What is the purpose of Bodhidharma's coming from the West?"

"Shhh! Too loud! Come closer," said Mazu.

Fahui came closer.

Mazu struck him and said, "We can't talk when there are six ears. Come again tomorrow."

The next day, Fahui entered the Dharma hall and said, "Pray, Master, speak—"

Mazu said, "Go and wait for now. Come back when I go up into the Dharma hall to give the Dharma talk. Then I'll show you."

At this, Fahui was enlightened and said, "Thank you, everyone, for showing me!" He walked a full circle around the Dharma hall and left.

渕潭法会禅師問祖云、如何是西来祖師意。祖曰、低声、近前来。会便近前。祖打一掴云、六耳不同謀。

来日来。会至来日、猶入法堂云、請和尚道。祖云、且
去、待老漢上堂時出来。与汝証明。会乃悟云、謝大
衆証明。乃繞法堂一帀便去。

If someone whispers to you to "come closer," you come closer. It's a conditioned response to a command that can leave you vulnerable, exposed. Fahui, without thinking, approaches Mazu—bam!

When Mazu says, "We can't talk when there are six ears," just to whom do these six ears belong?

The three people, it seems, would be Mazu, Fahui, and Bodhidharma. Mazu and Fahui have their own private space, so there's no room for a third party to enter. In spite of this, Fahui approaches eagerly, wanting to receive teachings about someone else. To make Fahui aware of his own brazen attitude, Mazu gives him a punch. "This isn't something you talk about with three people in a huddle together! You want to know about Bodhidharma? Go talk to him yourself." Fahui's question concerns no one but Bodhidharma and Fahui; there's no reason to involve a third party (Mazu) in the matter.

Mazu's kind offer to see him again tomorrow doesn't completely get through to Fahui. He takes his "Come again tomorrow" only at face value and visits again on the following day. The next day, when Fahui eagerly approaches again, Mazu's invitation to see the Dharma talk may be heard as "If you want to hear a Dharma talk, come along and listen when I'm speaking to everyone else as well. I'm just one person, and I don't go around teaching in secret."

This is the second time now that Mazu has tried to get rid of the dependent Fahui. It seems that the hardheaded Fahui finally gets it. He even leaves behind the admirable line, "Thank you, everyone, for showing me!" as he circles the Dharma hall and leaves. From here on, he's independent.

32

I Don't Feel Like It

A monk asked Mazu, "Pray, Master—apart from words and beyond reason, point directly to the meaning of Bodhidharma's coming from the West."

Mazu said, "I'm not in the mood today. Go and ask Zhizang."

The monk then asked Zhizang.

Zhizang said, "Why don't you ask Master Mazu?"

The monk said, "Master Mazu told me to come and ask you."

Zhizang rubbed his head with his hand and said, "I have a headache today. Go and ask Huaihai."

The monk went again and asked Huaihai.

Huaihai said, "I don't know."

The monk related these events to Mazu.

Mazu said, "Zhizang's head is white, Huaihai's head is black."

僧問祖云、請和尚、離四句絶百非、直指某甲西來意。
祖云、我今日無心情。汝去問取智蔵。其僧乃問蔵。蔵
云、汝何不問取和尚。僧云、和尚令某甲来問上座。
蔵以手摩頭云、今日頭痛。汝去問海師兄。其僧又去
問海。海云、我這裏却不会。僧乃挙似祖。祖云、蔵頭
白、海頭黒。

Having received the monk's ridiculous request to show the essential truth of Zen without any means of linguistic expression, Mazu says, "I'm not in the mood today. Go and ask Zhizang." And so the bowl is passed to Zhizang, who says, "I have a headache. Ask Huaihai." When Huaihai's turn comes, he just says, "I don't know."

Even though the question itself contained the request not to answer with your head, all three masters effectively dodge the question by blaming their heads: "my head is tired," "my head hurts," "my head isn't working." Each of the three, in his own way, is expressing the inexpressible. They are not just playing hot potato with the monk; Mazu, Zhizang, and Huaihai each answer the monk according to their own style.

And what about Mazu's comment that "Zhizhang's head is white, Huaihai's head is black"? The monk had requested an answer that transcends the divisions and categorizations inherent to language. It seems that Mazu is saying that there are ways of expressing even the unanswerable that can be classified as "white" or "black." Zhizang complains of a headache and asks to be excused. The way Zhizang's head works is symbolized by "white." Huaihai bluntly says, "I don't know," getting rid of the monk quite directly. Mazu calls the way Huaihai's head works "black." Perhaps when you are young, with black hair, you tend to use more energy and respond in more of a stern manner to evoke a reaction. As you age, as your hair turns white, you gradually take on a slightly different tone, something a bit more gentle. Both responses are equally valid, but they differ in tone and style.

The monk's request—"Apart from words and beyond reason . . ."—is a rather standard insistence in the Zen world. Let's take a look at a dialogue from *The Record of Zhaozhou*:

> Zhaozhou asked Nanquan, "Apart from words and beyond reason, pray speak—"
> Nanquan went right back to his quarters.
> Zhaozhou said, "This old priest! He's always flapping his mouth, but ask him a question and you don't get a single word!"
> The attendant monk said, "You shouldn't say that Master Nanquan said nothing."
> Zhaozhou slapped him.

"A word, please, on that which cannot be put into words." Hearing this, Nanquan hurries off to his quarters. Zhaozhou's response, "He's always yakking away, but here he couldn't even make a sound," is not directed at Nanquan. He means to provoke Nanquan's attendant. The attendant, off-guard, takes the bait and says, "Ah, but he *did* reply"—and so comes the obligatory slap.

The attendant is right, of course, in pointing out that the absence of speech does not necessitate the absence of communication. As soon as we put *that* into words, though, what happens to "apart from words and beyond reason"?

33

That's a Slippery Road!

Deng Yinfeng was about to take leave of Mazu.

Mazu said, "Where are you going?"

"To Shitou's."

Mazu said, "Shitou's road is slippery."

Yinfeng said, "As traveling performers carry a portable stage, I'll act as the situation demands." At that, he left.

As soon Yinfeng arrived at Shitou's, he went once around the master's seat, shook his staff, and asked, "Who are you?"

Shitou said, "Come now, come now!"

Yinfeng had nothing to say.

He went back and reported to Mazu.

Mazu said, "Go again, and when he says 'Come now, come now,' try sighing twice."

Yinfeng went again, and asked just as he had before.

Shitou let out two sighs.

Yinfeng again had nothing to say.

He returned and reported to Mazu.

Mazu said, "I told you Shitou's road was slippery."

隱峰辞祖。祖曰、甚処去。云、石頭去。祖曰、石頭路
滑。云、竿木随身、逢場作戲。便去。繞到石頭、乃遶
禪牀一匝、振錫一下問、是何宗旨。頭曰、蒼天蒼天。
峰無語。却回挙似祖。祖曰、汝更去、見他道蒼天蒼
天、汝便嘘両声。峰又去、一依前問。頭乃嘘両声。峰
又無語。帰挙似祖。祖曰、向汝道石頭路滑。

Mazu cautions Yinfeng: Shitou's teaching is quite difficult. If you go skipping on up to him like you don't
have a care in the world, you'll slip and fall flat on your
rear.

Mazu is advising Yinfeng that Shitou's Zen doesn't
even provide a foothold for understanding. His methods are severe, but it's a squishy, slippery brand of
severity, like a mountain of jelly—there's nothing to
grab hold of. Don't be fooled by Shitou's name, which
means "rock head."

Yinfeng is full of confidence, thinking he can easily
adjust to the needs of the moment. When he arrives
at Shitou's, he circles Shitou's seat and with a flourish
of his staff asks Shitou who he is, but Master Shitou's
response leaves him lost for words, unable to adapt to
the situation.

Yinfeng begs Mazu for help, and Mazu gives him
an idea: when Shitou says, "Come now, come now," as
though to say "What a boring question," let out two
sighs as if to say right back to him, "What a boring

answer." With this, maybe Yinfeng will be able to adapt to the situation this time.

Armed with Mazu's plan, Yinfeng sets off a second time to get his revenge. When he arrives, Shitou beats him to the punch and lets out two sighs. Robbed of his plans, Yinfeng again finds himself lost for words. So much for adapting to the situation, *again*. It looks like Shitou's Zen was too heavy for Yinfeng.

Beefing up your strength isn't going to help you climb when there's no foothold to begin with. You can only get a foothold on something that offers no foothold by means that don't involve getting a foothold.

Yinfeng seems to be basically a carrier pigeon; it's like Mazu and Shitou are sending him back and forth, using him to communicate with one another. You can fault him for his vain lack of self-awareness in thinking he could just adapt to the situation, but still, you feel sorry for him here.

34

Feeling Down

It was Master Shijiu's first visit to Mazu.

Mazu asked, "Where do you come from?"

Shijiu said, "From Wujiu."

Mazu said, "And what has Wujiu been saying these days?"

Shijiu said, "He says, 'How many people here are walking around in a daze.'"

Mazu said, "Forget dazed, what about depressed?"

Shijiu took three steps closer.

Mazu said, "I have seven staffs. I want to give Wujiu a thwack. Will you do it?"

Shijiu said, "You take the first blow. Then I'll do it."

At that, he returned to Wujiu.

石臼和尚初参祖。祖問、什麼処来。臼云、烏臼来。
祖云、烏臼近日有何言句。臼云、幾人於此茫然在。
祖云、茫然且置、悄然一句作麼生。臼乃近前三歩。

祖云、我有七棒。寄打烏臼。你還甘否。臼云、和尚先喫、某甲後甘。却回烏臼。

"How has Wujiu been doing lately?" asks Mazu. It seems he's concerned about how his disciple Wujiu is getting along since he left the nest.

Shijiu tells Mazu that many of the monks on the receiving end of Wujiu's methods, which are reportedly on the violent side, have become like zombies, walking around in a daze. "Even if we say that being dazed is no problem, what about being depressed?" responds Mazu. Just who is it that he thinks is depressed?

A plain reading tempts us to see that the monks are who he means. That is, after all the sudden beatings from Wujiu, they go from absent-minded to downright depressed. Mazu's "Maybe I'll let my seven sticks have a few words with him" is thus an offer given with rolled-up sleeves—an offer to stand in the place of Wujiu's downhearted, beaten pupils and give their teacher a bit of a thrashing of his own.

This reading might make us expect Mazu to be the one who ends up feeling depressed, since he was flatly rejected by Shijiu, but I don't think that's the case. I think Mazu intentionally provokes Shijiu to defend his teacher—and thus gives him a little encouragement. Not realizing what's going on, Shijiu tells Mazu to take a beating first, and turns smartly on his way home to Wujiu.

I wonder, though, if the one who's depressed here is actually Wujiu. Perhaps the dialogue shows Mazu empathizing with Wujiu, who must be feeling depressed himself what with all of his monks walking around like zombies after so many random beatings. In this reading, Mazu, while acknowledging the absent-minded monks, suggests to Shijiu that perhaps there is also someone who has lost spirit. Perhaps there is someone feeling discouraged. "I think there is," agrees Shijiu by taking three steps closer.

"Well, maybe I'll go and use my staff on Wujiu," replies Mazu, who then turns to Shijiu and asks, "Maybe you want to give it a go too, eh?"

But now it becomes clear that after all's said and done, Shijiu is still a Wujiu fan. "On the contrary, Master Mazu, I think you're the one who's going to get a thwack," says Shijiu. And with that, he leaves in a huff.

Shijiu is worried about Wujiu. Perceiving this, Mazu encourages Shijiu to give Wujiu some encouragement. But this prompts Shijiu to defend his teacher, and whether he's aware of Mazu's kindness or not, Shijiu becomes newly invigorated by turning down his offer. He promptly returns to Wujiu with his head held high.

If you just passively receive food all your life, you tend not to value it; as a child, you may even resist it, especially if it doesn't taste good. When you realize the value of what you're receiving, however, your perspective changes. When you realize that your body needs cabbage, you're more willing to eat it, even if it doesn't tickle your taste buds right away. Thanks to Mazu, Shijiu realizes that Wujiu wasn't simply hitting him for no reason; he was actually being taught something. Shijiu, newly encouraged, returns to Wujiu—this time, he's ready to receive what he's being taught. From a teacher's perspective, having students who are ready to receive your teaching is beneficial for your own confidence as well. Mazu manages to encourage both Wujiu and his caring pupil Shijiu in one fell swoop.

35

How Many Deer Can You Shoot with a Single Arrow?

Before he became a Zen master, Shigong Huizang was a huntsman and hated Buddhist priests. One day, while pursuing a herd of deer, he happened to pass in front of Mazu's residence. Mazu came out to meet him.

Huizang asked, "Master, have you seen some deer passing by?"

Mazu said, "Who are you?"

"A hunter."

Mazu said, "Can you shoot a bow?"

"I can shoot."

Mazu said, "How many deer can you shoot with one arrow?"

"One shot, one deer."

Mazu said, "You can't shoot."

"Can you shoot, Master?"

Mazu said, "I can shoot."

"How many can you shoot with one arrow?"

Mazu said, "One shot, one herd."

"Each one of them is a living being. How could you shoot an entire herd?"

Mazu said, "If you already know that, why haven't you shot yourself?"

"Even if I wanted to shoot myself, I don't know how to do it."

Mazu said, "In this man, ages of ignorance and desire have today been extinguished in an instant."

Huizang immediately broke his bow and arrows, shaved his head with his sword, and became a monk under Mazu.

石鞏慧藏禅師、本以弋猟為務、悪見沙門。因逐群鹿、従祖庵前過。祖乃迎之。蔵問、和尚見鹿過否。祖曰、汝是何人。曰、猟者。祖曰、汝解射否。曰、解射。祖曰、汝一箭射幾箇。曰、一箭射一箇。祖曰、汝不解射。曰、和尚解射否。祖曰、解射。曰、和尚一箭射幾箇。曰、一箭射一群。曰、彼此是命、何用射他一群。祖曰、汝既知如是、何不自射。曰、若教某甲自射、即無下手処。祖曰、這漢曠劫無明煩悩、今日頓息。蔵当時毀棄弓箭、自以刀截髪、投祖出家。

Huizang's occupation as a hunter puts him in opposition to Buddhist priests, for whom the destruction of life is forbidden. Deep inside, though, Huizang has conflicting feelings about what he's doing.

The way of a hunter is to kill one animal with one arrow. So long as they obtain enough food to sustain their life for the present, they're satisfied; they don't overhunt or kill what they can't use. The hunter's excellence comes through in his ability to exercise moderation.

The way of a Zen master is to kill a whole herd with one arrow. During a Dharma talk, they pierce the hearts of all who are present with a single word. To catch the whole school of fish in a single net is a Zen master's pride.

For Huizang, "shooting" means catching game; that is, to kill. For Mazu, "shooting" means waking people up. The hunter and the Zen master both use the same word, but for the former it means death while for the latter it means life.

"You can't shoot," says Mazu. At that, Mazu's "shoot" already carries a different meaning from that of Huizang, but Huizang doesn't realize it. That's why he blurts out a mindless question: "How many can you shoot with one arrow?" Mazu fires back: "One herd." Huizang still doesn't get it. "Each one of them is a living being," he says awkwardly.

His response shows that he does have compassion for them. Although he's killing, he has insight. The opportunity for enlightenment is present.

The opportunity ripens. "If you already know that, why haven't you shot yourself?" says Mazu. If you know the sanctity of life, then why don't you do something about the fact that you're a hunter who works at destroying it? Shouldn't your only target be the ignorance and passions of your own heart?

The hunter takes the life of a deer in order to nourish his own self. It's a necessary evil. In his head, he gets it; it's just that the haze over his conscience won't clear up. "If your conscience is so clouded, why don't you take a shot at your own life?" asks Mazu. "You've been thinking about nothing other than taking the lives of other beings; why don't you try taking your own? You can't save others unless you give up your own life."

Here Huizang gets it. The most important thing is to kill your own self. Mazu wastes no time in saying, "You finally got it!"

The hunter and the priest are diametrically opposed to one another. The priest must not kill; the hunter kills for a living. To the hunter, the priest is an enemy whose very existence is a threat to his own way of life.

However, the hunter is not killing recklessly. He would never pointlessly kill an entire herd of deer with a single arrow. That's who the hunter is.

Mazu jumps on that point. "You don't kill pointlessly. That's fine. But if that's who you are, why not shoot yourself? Then you won't have to kill any deer at all."

Huizang shoots and kills his hunter-self and is reborn as a Buddhist monk. Mazu leads him to be reborn as what would have been his own enemy.

Zen priests hit many targets with a single arrow. They are able to do such a thing only because the arrow is aimed at their very own self; they kill themselves and then come back to life. In doing this, they are able to bring many others back to life as well. The Zen priest's arrow is this: "To die is to live."

36

What Does It Mean to Attain the Way?

Someone asked Mazu, "What understanding must one have to be considered to have attained the Way?"

Mazu said, "You are yourself. If you just keep from getting caught up over good and evil, you have already mastered the Way. Doing good and rejecting evil, discerning emptiness and working toward samadhi—this is all useless striving. If you go about searching for the Way externally, the more you search the further away it grows. Give up trying to grasp the world with your mind. Striving with your mind is the root of suffering. Just keep from striving, and you'll be able to remove all suffering. This is obtaining the Dharma King's most precious treasure.

又問、作何見解、即得達道。祖曰、自性本来具足。
但於善悪事中不滞、喚作修道人。取善捨悪、観空入

定、即属造作。更若向外馳求、転疎転遠。但尽三界
心量。一念妄心、即是三界生死根本。但無一念、即
除生死根本、即得法王無上珍宝。

The question is nonsense. No matter what answer you
get, can you ever finally say, "Ah, so this is what attaining the Way looks like"?

In Buddhist practice, it's useless to have someone else tell you the answers. Attaining the Way is
not something that can be described objectively, like
a series of facts. As such, the question above doesn't
even qualify as an answerable question; Mazu has no
way to respond. Still, it turns out that Mazu answers
just beautifully.

He begins by declaring that your way of being
already exists complete within you. No matter what
happens, you're always going to be yourself. Accept
yourself just as you are.

The statements "I am six feet tall" and "I like taking
walks" are fundamentally different. You can do nothing about the fact that you are six feet tall. Whether or
not you like taking walks, though, is for you to decide.
You may be able to ask someone else, "Excuse me, can
you measure me to see if my height is indeed six feet?"
but it would be beyond stupid to ask, "Tell me, do I like
taking walks?" As far as things that you yourself must
decide are concerned, seeking the standard outside of
yourself is to no avail.

Say that you have decided that you are yourself.
Here, the question of understanding simply does not
apply. Deciding and understanding are incompatible.

When you understand something, you are recognizing preexisting facts (and thus it is possible to be incorrect). When you decide, your decision creates a new fact (and thus there is no way for you to be incorrect).

Attaining the Way is not accomplished by reaching an objective path, a Way, that happens to be in a certain place. You have to discern for yourself: "Okay. *This* is the Way." It's not something that, explained by someone or something outside of you, you have to understand, as in "Ah, so *this* is the Way."

When it comes to external things, whether or not a certain road happens to be "the way" to the grocery store, for example, must be determined objectively. But when it comes to your own discernment that "This is the Way," if someone else tells you that it's not, you can just let it roll off your back; their words have no weight at all. That's why "If you go about searching for the Way externally, the more you search the further away it grows."

You're not going to find any external grounds for the fact that you are yourself. This world is your world; there's no way around it, no other way to be. As far as this way of being goes, no particular "understanding" is possible, nor is it necessary.

Mind is mind, and Buddha is Buddha. Still, there is no Buddha other than mind. Mind and Buddha are not-two. That's why Mazu says to accept yourself, your ordinary mind, here and now—just as you are. To do this is to live as Buddha; it's none other than the Way.

Conclusion

Zen dialogues, by nature, include the "I and Thou" relationship—a living, subjective experience in which "you" and "I" are not separate from one another. This must not, however, be a "master and servant" relationship wherein the disciple asks for teaching and the master supplies the answer. It can only be the direct, here-and-now collision of individual personalities, of equals.

The disciple and teacher are engaged in a dialogue—just as we have been in this book. I'm sure Mazu has helped us all realize a few things that might have been difficult to see on our own. Even if you are a student, you can't just passively hand the leadership over to your teacher. As a disciple, you run up against your teacher with your own true self, comparable to no one. You may end up feeling deflated, of course, but that's okay.

Someone asks Mazu, "What understanding must one have to be considered to have attained the Way?" Mazu replies that the Way is to be yourself; there's no need to trouble yourself with mastering anything. If you see that your ordinary mind is the Way, and you encounter every "thou" by being the "I" that you are, then you've already attained the Way.

Appendix 1: The Life and Teachings of Master Mazu

Originally published in *Zen's Chinese Heritage* by Andy Ferguson

MAZU DAOYI (709–88) was a student of Nanyue Huairang. After Huineng, Mazu is the most famous of the ancient Chinese Zen masters. Two of the traditionally acknowledged major schools of Zen trace their lineage through this renowned Zen ancient. From his home in Sichuan Province, Mazu made his way to Zhongqing, where he initially studied under a second-generation student of Daman Hongren (the Fifth Ancestor). There he received ordination as a Buddhist monk. Later, he settled on Mt. Heng, where he met Nanyue Huairang. After ten years of study with Nanyue, he received Dharma transmission, then proceeded to travel as a *yunshui* the length and breadth of China, perfecting his understanding of the Buddha Way. Eventually he settled at Zhongling (now Nanchang City), where students from every quarter came to study with him.

Mazu's Zen lineage is remembered as the Hongzhou Zen school. Located in what is now Jiangxi Province, it was the dominant Zen school of the later Tang dynasty (late ninth and early tenth centuries). Mazu was the first Zen teacher acknowledged to use the staff to jolt his students into awakening. The strident style of his Hongzhou school foreshadowed the uncompromising training methods of his famous Zen descendant, Linji Yixuan.

Unlike some other Zen masters of his time, Mazu did not leave an extensive written record of his teachings. Instead, we know of him largely from imaginative legends that reflect the awesome sense of presence that he conveyed.

Like the great Zen masters of all ages, Mazu emphasized the immediacy of Zen enlightenment. He emphasized the teaching that "mind is Buddha" and "This place is itself true thusness." Mazu's "sudden" approach moved the Chinese spiritual scales back toward "pointing directly at mind," the essential teaching of Bodhidharma's Zen.

The acclaimed greatness of a Zen master does not arise simply from his or her message. Equally important is the awesome and bone-chilling presence that such masters demonstrate. This tangible sense of presence reveals an astonishing freedom. Zen students, observing such masters, naturally aspire to gain the remarkable composure, effortless grace, and uncluttered vision that they embody. Later generations gain a sense of what these ancients were like partly through their words, but more intimately through their legends.

The *Wudeng Huiyuan* provides the following account of Mazu's life and teaching:

Zen Master Mazu Daoyi of Jiangxi was from Shifang in Hanzhou [about forty kilometers north of the modern city of Chengdu in Sichuan Province]. His surname was Ma. He entered Luohan Temple in his home district. His appearance was most unusual. He strode like an ox and glared like a tiger. His extended tongue covered his nose. On the soles of his feet his veins formed two circles. As a youth he received tonsure under a monk named Tang in Zizhou. He was fully ordained under Vinaya master Yuan in Yu Province.

During the Kai Yuan era [713–41] Mazu met Master Nanyue Huairang while practicing Zen meditation on Mt. Heng. Six others also studied with Nanyue but only Mazu received the secret mind seal. Nanyue Huairang and his student Mazu Daoyi can be compared with Qingyuan Xingsi and his student Shitou Xiqian. Though they came from the same source, they diverged into two branches. The brilliance of ancient Zen arose through these two masters. Liu Ke said, "In Jiangxi is Master Daji. In Hunan is Master Shitou. Anyone traversing the country seeking a teacher who doesn't see these two will remain ignorant."

The record of Prajnadhara of India made a prediction about Bodhidharma, saying, "Although the great land of China is vast, there are no roads where my descendants won't travel. The phoenix, with a single grain, nourishes the saints and monks in the ten directions."

The Sixth Ancestor [also citing an ancient prediction by Prajnadhara] said to Nanyue, "Hereafter, from the area to which you will go, a horse will come forth and trample everyone in the world to death."

Later, the Dharma of Nanyue's spiritual heir was spread across the world. People of that time called him Master Ma.

From Buddha Trace Mountain in Jianyang, Mazu moved to Linchuan. He then moved to Nankang at Gonggong Mountain. In the middle of the Dali era [766–79], Mazu lived at the Kaiyuan Temple in Zhongling. During that time the high official Lu Sigong heard of Mazu's reputation and personally came to receive instruction. Because of this, students from the four quarters gathered like clouds beneath Mazu's seat.

Appendix 2: Lineage of Zen Patriarchs in China Mentioned in This Book

(Japanese names are in parentheses.)

Appendix 2: Lineage of Zen Patriarchs in China

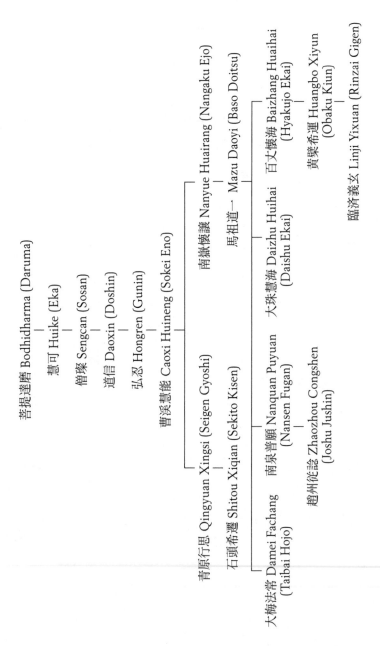

菩提達磨 Bodhidharma (Daruma)

慧可 Huike (Eka)

僧璨 Sengcan (Sosan)

道信 Daoxin (Doshin)

弘忍 Hongren (Gunin)

曹溪慧能 Caoxi Huineng (Sokei Eno)

南嶽懷讓 Nanyue Huairang (Nangaku Ejo)

馬祖道一 Mazu Daoyi (Baso Doitsu)

大珠慧海 Daizhu Huihai (Daishu Ekai)

百丈懷海 Baizhang Huaihai (Hyakujo Ekai)

黄檗希運 Huangbo Xiyun (Obaku Kiun)

臨済義玄 Linji Yixuan (Rinzai Gigen)

青原行思 Qingyuan Xingsi (Seigen Gyoshi)

石頭希遷 Shitou Xiqian (Sekito Kisen)

南泉普願 Nanquan Puyuan (Nansen Fugan)

趙州従諗 Zhaozhou Congshen (Joshu Jushin)

大梅法常 Damei Fachang (Taibai Hojo)

Index of Names

(excluding Mazu Daoyi)

About the Author

 Dr. Fumio Yamada was born in Fukui, Japan, in 1959. He graduated from Tohoku University with a PhD in literature and currently works as a professor of Chinese Classics at Hirosaki University. He is also a designated lineage holder of Kinpu-ryu, Hirosaki's unique school of *shakuhachi* (the Zen flute), which is one of Japan's intangible cultural treasures.

He is the author of more than ten publications in Japanese, with topics ranging from Dogen Zenji to Lao Tzu, as well as Confucius, Sun Tzu, *The Gateless Gate*, and other classical Chinese and Japanese texts.

About the Translator

John "Nick" Bellando was born in New Jersey and currently lives in Hirosaki, Japan, with his wife Mutsumi and daughters Emma and May. He holds a BS in Biblical studies and an MA in Japanese education / Chinese literature from Hirosaki University, where he studied under Dr. Yamada. He writes, translates, and makes shakuhachi. Visit him online at www.hon-on.com.

What to Read Next
from Wisdom Publications

Zen's Chinese Heritage
The Masters and Their Teachings
Andy Ferguson
Forewords by Reb Anderson and Steven Heine

"This is an indispensable reference for any student of Buddhism. Ferguson has given us an impeccable and very readable translation."—John Daido Loori, late abbot, Zen Mountain Monastery

Zen
The Authentic Gate
Koun Yamada
Foreword by David R. Loy

"Yamada's introduction to Zen is a welcome and dense primer that has much to offer novices as well as experienced practitioners."—*Publishers Weekly*

The Gateless Gate
The Classic Book of Zen Koans
Koun Yamada
Foreword by Ruben L. F. Habito

"Yamada Roshi's straightforward commentary on the *Wu-men kuan* (*Mumonkan*) is again available in this new edition, and I'm delighted."—Robert Aitken, author of *Zen Master Raven*

The Zen Teachings of Homeless Kodo
Kosho Uchiyama and Shohaku Okumura
Edited by Molly Delight Whitehead

"Kodo Sawaki was straight-to-the-point, irreverent, and deeply insightful—and one of the most influential Zen teachers for us in the West. I'm very happy to see this book."—Brad Warner, author of *Hardcore Zen*

Novice to Master
An Ongoing Lesson in the Extent of My Own Stupidity
Soko Morinaga
Translated by Belenda Attaway Yamakawa

"This wise and warm book should be read by all."
—Anthony Swofford, author of *Jarhead*

The Book of Equanimity
Illuminating Classic Zen Koans
Gerry Shishin Wick
Foreword by Bernie Glassman

"Every student of Zen would do well to read this fine book."—Robert Jinsen Kennedy, author of *Zen Spirit, Christian Spirit*

The Record of Transmitting the Light
Zen Master Keizan's Denkoroku
Translated and introduced by Francis Dojun Cook
Foreword by John Daido Loori

"Both Keizan's text itself and Dr. Cook's superb introduction are invaluable in studying our Zen lineage."—Zenkei Blanche Hartman, Abbess, San Francisco Zen Center

About Wisdom Publications

Wisdom Publications is the leading publisher of classic and contemporary Buddhist books and practical works on mindfulness. To learn more about us or to explore our other books, please visit our website at wisdompubs.org or contact us at the address below.

Wisdom Publications
199 Elm Street
Somerville, MA 02144 USA

We are a 501(c)(3) organization, and donations in support of our mission are tax deductible.

Wisdom Publications is affiliated with the Foundation for the Preservation of the Mahayana Tradition (FPMT).